A Practical Guide to Becoming an RN and Surviving Your First Year

NURSES' STATION 101:

The FRONTLINE, FLATLINES, and BURNOUT

Robert L. Greene, BSN, RN, CPAN

ISBN: 978-0-57886-654-3 Print
ISBN: 978-1-09836-766-4 eBook

DISCLAIMER

*Clinical scenarios in this text are based upon fictitious characters

Although the author has made every effort to ensure that the information
in this book was correct at press time, the author does not assume and hereby
disclaim any liability to any party for any loss, damage, or disruption
caused by errors or omissions, whether such errors or omissions
result from negligence, accident, or any other cause.

To my greatest loves: Leo, Roberta, Charlie, and Donna.

A special shout out to "Messy" G.I. Jessie,
whose quest for knowledge drove me to drink...
Don't ever stop asking questions.

... oh, and I mustn't forget my first nursing instructor
who introduced me to an anal wink
for the very first time. To this day, you are
the inspiration for my practice in the G.I. Lab.

"Prepare the child for the road,
not the road for the child."

—origin unknown

CONTENTS

Did I Really Sign Up for This?

It's 05:00 a.m., dark outside, and I'm still half asleep. As I walked down the hall to the elevator to report to my unit, I was overwhelmed with that familiar smell of the hospital that I never got used to during all of my clinical rotations in nursing school. That hospital smell. What was it? Probably the industrial chemicals that are used to cover up fluids and smells that are hard to cover up. It was kind of unsettling to me. Well, it was a familiar smell that lingered in my nose and caused a bit of anxiety because it reminded me of where I was, and that I finally made it. Each new day that I walked down that hall I was reminded that I was not a nursing student anymore but a newbie registered nurse. A registered nurse with a full six months of critical acute care hospital experience. Wow! I made the six-month mark. Having just graduated from my program with high honors, I thought I might know a thing or two and that I would conquer the world of 6 North, which was a very progressive step-down open-heart unit located in a level one regional trauma center, and it was also my very first job as a brand-new nurse.

On this day, I felt more anxious than I usually felt reporting to my unit. It was my first time being in charge. I felt overwhelmed with this responsibility that was suddenly thrust upon me. I kept overanalyzing why they put me in charge as a very new nurse in a very critical unit. Was it because I was a male in a profession dominated by females? Oh no, that would be construed as sexist, right? Was it because I was smart or serious about doing the job? Maybe, it was because they just didn't have anybody else that wanted to do it. Nevertheless, today it was on me. Who knows why I was chosen, but it was my job and I had to stay focused. I made a concentrated effort to keep my hands from shaking as I made the assignment. I didn't feel like I knew enough to be in charge. In an instant, a million worst-case scenarios flashed through my head. What if I didn't assign a nurse to a patient and the patient didn't receive care, or important treatments were delayed, or worse yet, completely missed. I kept running scenarios in my head as I tried to focus on the task at hand. Anyway, our patients were critical, and I had to keep in mind their acuity levels while also focusing on our staffing ratios, skill mix of the staff, ancillary personnel, late calls, sick calls, etcetera.

Our surgery program averaged about seven hundred open hearts per year. The step-down unit that I worked in was directly connected to the heart surgical intensive care unit (ICU), and many patients were "fast-tracked" out of the ICU to us. These patients were often transferred with their atrial and ventricular wires coming out of their chest so that in an emergency, we could connect them to a digital external pacemaker. Many times, our patients were transferred to us with their wires already connected to the pacemaker. In this instance, in a handoff report, we were notified that sometimes the patient had no underlying heart rhythm and that they were totally dependent on the functioning of this pacer and on the nurse's vigilance in monitoring the patient. Oh yeah, we were really very serious about getting a good report and knowing the functionality of these external digital pacers. They reminded me of those big bulky cell phones from the eighties, except these bulky devices were attached directly to patients' hearts, so you don't really want a dropped call if you know what I mean. Always know where the backup batteries are and what button to push for the asynchronous pacing mode!

Okay, back to the assignment that I had made. Every patient was assigned a nurse. Check. Followed nurse-patient ratio guidelines. Check. Monitored for sick calls, so far there was none. Check. Wow! This was not so bad. My hands stopped shaking, and I perceived some silence and calm at the nursing station. The evening nurses were in rooms delivering their last medications and ordered treatments. As I paused to look up at the assignment board to triple check my work, I heard a nursing assistant scream from the patient room directly across from where I was standing. She screamed and she screamed loud: "Help! Help!" I felt my anxiety return one hundred-fold, except this time my anxiety was fueled by pure adrenaline coursing through my veins. As I ran toward the room, I could feel the intense heat from my face as I began to get flushed.

My heart started to pound. This was no ordinary pounding; it felt as though I could feel my heartbeat in my throat. As I entered the room, I saw the nursing assistant fruitlessly trying to prop up a patient that was lying on his right side, facing me. I didn't hesitate as I moved quickly into the room toward the patient. The room was dark. As I moved in closer, I could see that the patient's monitor was off. His telemetry pack was lying on the floor. I started to be able see the patient's color. He was blue. And as everyone is aware, blue skin and blue lips are not a good color for a person unless you are working in Vegas with the Blue Man Group. As I approached the patient, it was obvious that he was not breathing. I leaned into him to assess for a carotid pulse as I simultaneously darted for the code blue button behind him. I pushed the button and set the alarm off. He was still warm as I was trying to find his pulse. I did not feel one. The nursing assistant continued to yell for help as the code blue alarm was flashing and ringing in concert with her cries for help. This was disconcerting, to say the least. I yelled to the nursing assistant to grab the crash cart, and her response was to stand still and continue to yell for help. I struggled to turn the patient to a supine position. I started cardiopulmonary resuscitation (CPR) while thinking, where is the code team?! It felt like an absolute eternity. Why was no one else here? Why was no one responding to this code? The code blue alarm siren felt absolutely deafening to me, somebody must have heard it. And I can't imagine that somebody could not hear the screaming nursing assistant. She was louder than the code blue siren. Finally, as I continued compressions, a very experienced heart surgical respiratory therapist came in with the crash cart. He started to give me directives. He seemed calm and nervous at the same time. Is that even possible? His hands were not visibly shaking as mine were. He directed me that he would continue CPR and that I would need to attach the patient to our crash cart monitor. I attached the patient to the monitor, then I quickly kept checking the connections because I could not see a rhythm on my screen. The respiratory therapist firmly reminded me that I needed to turn the monitor on. Oh yeah, right. So, I did while uninterrupted CPR was in progress. We paused to check the patient's rhythm. I, as a new registered nurse, had very recently completed my Advanced Cardiac Life Support (ACLS) certification. I needed that certification to work in this unit. Through that certification, cardiac treatment algorithms were drilled into our heads. We relentlessly reviewed our rhythm strips so that we could easily identify what these life-threatening dysrhythmias looked like. But studying those rhythms in a book and seeing it in real life right in front of you was a totally brand-new experience for me. What I was seeing on that monitor, I could very easily identify. But this time, that monitor was attached to a human being and not a simulation device. It was very clearly ventricular fibrillation, up close and in person. I had a sudden epiphany. This person was technically dead. The rhythm on the screen wasn't a simulation; it was coming from the man lying in front of me. This was someone's relative. Someone's father, brother, or husband. It was very clear—he needed our interventions immediately. Ventricular fibrillation is an unorganized heart rhythm that does not produce any cardiac output, meaning no pulse, and the first line of treatment to convert ventricular fibrillation into an organized life-giving heartbeat is defibrillation. The respiratory therapist looked at the screen, then looked at me, and said, "You need to shock him. You need to shock him now." Back in the day, our crash cart brand was the "Code Master." It was a bright-yellow monophasic defibrillator with the old-school paddles that were more commonly used at the time, and we delivered what was called stacked shocks, meaning three stacked shocks that ranged from a dose of 200 joules up to 360 joules. The level of joules equates to the defibrillation dose or the amount of the electrical current you are going to administer to the patient's heart. As I was looking to set the appropriate joules on the turn knob, the respiratory therapist exclaimed to turn the knob all the way up to the right and hit the charge button. My hands were shaking even worse now, but I was able to maintain my composure and do just that. He continued to instruct me to pick up the paddles and apply them to the patient's chest while not touching the patient. He kept repeating to hit the charge button. "Hit the charge button!" he repeatedly droned. I did as I synchronously applied the paddles to his right upper chest and the apex of his heart. I strained to see through the profuse sweat falling off my forehead all the while listening to that escalating sound the machine makes when it is actively charging. He then emphatically said to shock him. He continued to instruct me to press the two buttons located on the top of the paddles. "Lean into it, don't touch the patient, and press the buttons now!" I did. I felt the energy in my hands, discharge from the machine into the patient. The patient's body twitched and contracted. It wasn't like in the movies, it was much subtler. It was a sensation I had never felt before in my life. I looked at the patient, then to the monitor. By this time, the room was full. There was a team here. It felt I was seeing everything in slow motion as someone moved into me to get epinephrine from the crash cart. The respiratory therapist who had guided me was now assisting with intubation at the head of the bed. Multiple people were speaking to me in slow motion all at once in what seemed like a very obscure Chinese dialect, and I don't speak Chinese. I saw everything in slow motion, but it was all happening so fast. It wasn't like this at all in my Advanced Cardiac Life Support class. This was a lot more challenging. Oh yeah, this was real life, and there were a lot more variables to consider. We repeated the ACLS algorithm over and over again. We secured the patient's airway, continued compressions, and administered epinephrine. Shock, compressions, epinephrine. Shock, compressions, and epinephrine. We continued this process until the patient had a return of spontaneous circulation. We brought the patient back to the cardiothoracic ICU, which was just one door down. It was now 07:00 a.m. The day staff was coming in and I couldn't remember if I had made the assignment! I wondered out loud, "How many hours are left in this shift?"

Fast Forward 25 Years and about 47,000 Clinical Practice Hours Later

Honestly, that experience in the open-heart unit over 20 years ago was just a typical day for a registered nurse working in an acute care hospital setting. I just didn't know that could be considered a typical day. That experience was the norm and still is. What was not mentioned in my introduction to 6 North as a new nurse was all of the other variables involved in daily practice such as policy and politics, patient acuity levels, nurse to patient ratios, hospital and department budgets, staffing shortages (which many times were intentional by the administration), and other factors that contribute to the highly challenging environment that the nurse must face on a daily basis when advocating for a patient. None of those factors have changed since my initial introduction to practicing as a registered nurse. In fact, those factors and challenges have been compounded and have exponentially grown. The healthcare system in the United States is highly complex and the delivery of healthcare is often fragmented at best. People need advocacy. Ultimately, we will all become consumers of healthcare. Yes, everyone will need these vital services in their lifetime. This leads me to question why a developed nation such as ours has not come up with a plan to provide this basic inalienable right for all of its citizens. Is it because certain factions of our political society think that healthcare is a privilege? These political factions are seemingly untouchable and out of touch with people like you and me. Our current convoluted politicking has impeded our ability as a civilized society to care for its own. This is unconscionable. The political tear in the fabric of our society has daily and long-lasting repercussions to our patients and hardworking frontline nurses, doctors, caregivers, and hospital staff. Oh, and yes, all this politicking and the impact it has on our healthcare providers and patients is relevant to the current status of our healthcare delivery system but is beyond the scope of this book. But always keep it in the back of your mind because one day, it will affect your practice and our survival, figuratively and literally. Welcome to your journey.

CHAPTER 1

A Nurse Is a Nurse Is a Nurse: Not!

Before we discuss the entry into practice for becoming a nurse, let's define what a registered nurse is. When I was overwhelmed doing my prerequisites for the nursing program I had chosen (I believe I was taking microbiology at the time), a "friend" who was studying to get her master's in library science said to me, "Oh, so you're gonna be a nurse. So, what does that mean? When you finally graduate, you will be able to give a shot and wipe a butt?" LOL! Well, I can attest that after some 47,000 clinical hours in a hospital I have done both. But it is important to note the broad misunderstanding of the general public regarding the role and scope of practice of a professionally licensed registered nurse. As a student or a new nurse, you yourself may not have a clear idea of what your newly minted role is. So, what's a nurse? According to Merriam-Webster dictionary, the definition of a registered nurse is a graduate trained nurse who has been licensed by a state authority after qualifying for registration. Really? That's it? Well, honestly, the complex and vast scope of practice of registered nurses and advanced practice nurses is well beyond the scope of this book. But I will attempt to give you a more comprehensive definition of what a nurse is. The American Nurses Association (ANA, 2015) cites *Nursing's Social Policy Statement, Second Edition*'s definition of nursing as follows, "Nursing is the protection, promotion, and optimization of health and abilities, prevention of illness and injury, facilitation of healing, alleviation of suffering through the diagnosis and treatment of human response, and advocacy in the care of individuals, families, groups, communities, and populations." This definition is the culmination of the mastery of the nurse clinician in synthesizing formal education, clinical tasks, and critical thinking. The mastery of each of these categories is essential to the other. You cannot protect, promote, and optimize health without the mastery of formal education, clinical practice, and critical thinking. This process does include being able to master clinical tasks, but the mastery of tasks alone does not constitute a professional registered nurse. In relation to clinical tasks, the registered nurse must be aware of his or her scope of practice. Would you allow a person who wanted to be a nurse or doctor but hasn't actually gone to school yet administer medication to you? How about a person who dreamed of becoming a veterinarian who did not study veterinary medicine but just loves dogs? Would you let them perform surgery on your pup? Licensing of healthcare providers helps to assure public safety. Each nurse who practices is governed by the Nurse Practice Act (NPA) of their state. Another layer to how you define what a registered nurse is relates to their scope of practice. Nurse Practice Acts are actual state laws, and your state Board of Nursing (BON) will interpret and enforce those legislative rules defined by the state. So, you must be aware of these laws in your particular state. The ANA (2015) notes the standards of professional nursing practice as statements of the duties that all registered nurses across all specialties and populations are expected to perform competently. These standards of practice for the professional nurse represent the nursing process which is considered to be a critical thinking model. So, the registered nurse is not only licensed to perform simple to highly complex tasks but is responsible to utilize scientific models such as the nursing process to guide autonomous nurse decision making. The nursing process model is the basis of our professional practice. The ANA (2015) notes the nursing process model utilizes the scientific components of assessment, diagnosis, planning, implementation, and evaluation. The nurse's evaluation is paramount to the collection of significant data when assessing a patient in their current situation. The nurse analyzes assessment data to determine actual or potential problems. The nurse also engages in planning, implementation, and evaluation of data to identify expected outcomes for the patient. This is a scientific process that is not necessarily dependent upon the mere performance of a task. What does that mean? That means the professional nurse is not only defined as an individual licensed to perform certain tasks as defined by the NPA and interpreted by the BON, but the nurse is responsible to critically understand the implications and outcomes of executing these tasks and how they may impact patient well-being. The ANA (2015) notes a professional nurse is further defined by the standards of professional performance. These standards define a competent level of professional performance demonstrated by the nurse. The standards include the ethical practice of the nurse, interprofessional communication and collaboration among different medical disciplines, and consistently demonstrating culturally congruent practice. The standard for nurse leadership and continuing formal education is essential to modern practice in all healthcare settings. Finally, the standard that most represents the evolution of modern professional nursing practice is the professional nurse's commitment to integrate evidence-based practice and research findings into daily practice. I am emphasizing the standard of evidence-based practice as to how we define what a registered nurse is. One day you will be a preceptor, mentor, and leader to others who are entering the profession. Long gone are the days when a colleague or a student asks you the rationale for what you are doing and you respond with "Well, that's just how we all have done it for years." Just doing something for years does not constitute an evidence-based practice. Get used to these concepts. Your practice should be data-driven. The simple execution of tasks is not so simple. They should be based upon evidence-based practice guidelines. Why you practice the way you practice must have an evidence-driven rationale. You will also need to speak to that rationale, understand that rationale, and ultimately contribute to policy that embodies evidence-based rationales. That, my friend, is a very brief explanation of what a registered nurse is.

Entry into Practice: ADN versus BSN/MSN

Associate of Science Degree, Bachelor of Science Degree, or Master of Science Degree, which one? We'll see. But first, I would like to introduce the concepts of "Filling Your Toolbox," and "Knowing Who You Are." These concepts relate to acquiring as much formal education and as many certifications as possible to be marketable to an employer in the highly competitive healthcare sector. Today's healthcare setting has become extremely complex, and there is an exponential increase in the use of modern technological innovation to aid in the delivery of care. What does this have to do with you becoming a registered nurse? Well, the answer is everything. The Institute of Medicine (IOM) has recommended that the entry into professional nursing practice should be at a minimum of a baccalaureate degree. In the modern healthcare setting, there is increased emphasis on evidence-based practice, interprofessional collaboration and collegiality, and a team-based approach to safe and effective patient care. There is an emphasis that all professions raise the bar for their educational preparation. At one time in our past, pharmacists were prepared at the bachelor's level, but in our current complex healthcare delivery system, many organizations seek to hire pharmacists that are educationally prepared at the doctorate level. How does this affect our pool of competent and motivated students that cannot afford to start out in such a program? There are many smart, dedicated, and motivated students that do not have the opportunity to begin their path to becoming a professional nurse at the baccalaureate level. But the fact of the matter is that in the current employment environment, organizations namely Magnet organizations, seek to hire only baccalaureate-prepared nurses. So, what do you do?

Entry into the profession via a three-year diploma is virtually nonexistent. There are many associate degree programs available, but as an inexperienced new grad, it will be extremely competitive to obtain a desired hospital job. A common misconception at the associate level is that you may complete this degree in a two-year time frame. This is impossible. Even if you are not working and devote a full-time schedule to your schooling, you will not complete your degree within a two-year time frame. It is required that you take basic essential classes on anatomy and physiology 1&2, chemistry, pharmacology, microbiology, and other prerequisites prior to even gaining admission into the actual nursing program. This will take time and is not only dependent upon your personal schedule but on class and instructor availability at the institutional level. Even at the associate degree level, competition has increased dramatically. The curriculum has always been rigorous, but competition is stiffer than ever. You will have to maintain a minimum 3.0 GPA with your prerequisite studies to even be considered for entry into the program. That may not sound too crazy, but these are hard science courses, and it will take huge discipline to study consistently to maintain your GPA. These programs emphasize heavy clinical rotations in different specialties along with the didactic portion of the rotation. Associate programs have always been impacted due to a lack of professors, and in our current pandemic environment, the situation has obviously gotten worse. There are currently waiting lists to get into associate degree programs. On average, you will need three years to complete your associate degree in nursing. If you are accepted into an associate degree program, the work has just begun. Anecdotally speaking, approximately 50 percent of the students who start this program do not make it to graduation.

There are many Bachelor of Science degree programs to choose from. There are RN to BSN degrees for nurses already licensed to practice as RNs. There are prelicensure BSN programs, some of which are accelerated and may be completed in three years. These programs not only contain the requisite hard science courses as described earlier but heavily focus on evidence-based practice and theory. There is much more concentration on taking the information learned from hard science courses and synthesizing that information into critical analysis papers. There is a great emphasis on how to retrieve evidence-based literature, how to examine that literature and make practical applications of that literature to formulate evidenced-based practice guidelines to measurably improve patient outcomes. Now you may ask why you would need to know how to reference all of this peer-reviewed literature. How is that gonna make me a better nurse? My response is that I believe this will enhance your practice as a nurse. Will it make you better at shooting a cardiac output on a Swan-Ganz catheter? Probably not. Will it make you better at understanding the whole picture? I believe it will. For decades in clinical practice, I have heard old-timers like myself moan and groan about advancing their formal education. "Why in hell would

I get another degree? I'm already a registered nurse with the exact same license as someone with a master's!" I have heard others exclaim, "That bonehead with the master's degree can't even put in a Foley!" I must admit I was one of those nurses! It has been a focal point for years among experienced associate-level clinicians watching their BSN counterparts struggle to acclimate themselves clinically. It must be noted that whether your entry into practice is at the associate, baccalaureate, or master's level, there will always be a learning curve. Integrating theory with clinical practice takes time no matter what your preparation, so I say there is no substitute for years of clinical experience. No matter what your formal degree, it will take time and practice to become a competent clinician.

What does this mean for you? Is an associate degree a dead end in this current and evolving healthcare setting? The answer is absolutely not. This is a very viable choice even with the shift of moving to the baccalaureate degree as a minimum point of entry into the profession. But I must emphasize that you will have to examine "who you are." That means taking into consideration your own personal circumstances. What is your budget? Do you have kids? What is your timeline for completing your degree? How much will it cost? These are just but a few very important personal factors in making your decision. I personally believe that to collectively advance as a profession we must all be engaged in continuing our formal education regardless of the degree we choose as our entry into practice. I know you have heard that by choosing to pursue an associate degree, it will be extremely difficult to get the desirable hospital job that you want. I believe this to be true in the current environment, especially with the goal of many hospital organizations to obtain Magnet status. But if choosing the associate path suits who you are and makes the most sense to you, I say you must go for it. Once you have completed the associate degree and have passed your licensure examination, you will need to apply immediately into an RN to BSN program. The National Council Licensure Examination (NCLEX-RN), as you probably know, is a nationwide examination for the licensing of nurses in the United States. Regardless of your initial degree, whether it be associate, baccalaureate, or master's, this is the exam you will take. Remember, there is no quick path to the goal. Only the path that makes the most sense for you!

THE COST OF EDUCATION: WHAT IS GOING ON?!

Ok, so we have discussed various degrees for entry into the nursing profession, but what's it gonna cost? There are many types of nursing programs across the United States, from community colleges to public and private universities. Take great time to independently research your path to entry into the profession. I must emphasize to you "Buyer Beware!" I say this because I have noticed great trends in the cost of education that have astounded me. People say you cannot put a price on education, but you must! Especially if you do not have Lori Loughlin's bucks or you are not trending on Insta like Olivia Jade. No shade to Olivia Jade! No, really. Your decision on how much you spend and how much you finance will have a huge impact on your financial health in the future.

Community colleges are the most reasonable option, but as I have stated, they are currently hugely impacted. It would be well worth researching those opportunities in your local area. Remember, if that's your path and it makes fiscal and life sense to you, then, by all means, pursue that path but plan on enrolling in an RN to BSN program after completion. There isn't really a straightforward answer to what nursing school costs because there are so many different pathways to achieve this education. On average, it is noted that community college will run you around $20,000 for an associate degree, and private universities may charge $40,000 for this same degree. I gotta tell you, guys, if you find these opportunities for entry into practice with an associate degree, then take them because currently the trend in obtaining a baccalaureate degree dominates the market and will cost you a whopping $100,000 to $140,000! Yes, $140,000 for a BSN! Remember what I said: "Buyer Beware!" Well, if you are going to invest $140,000 at a private for-profit university, you need to do a return-on-investment analysis for yourself. This analysis will include the total cost of your education including finance rates and the term of the loan. Is this a second career for you? How long do you anticipate that you will work in the profession in order to pay back the loan? Of course, you need to have an idea of what the salary is for a registered nurse. According to the Bureau of Labor Statistics (BLS), registered nurses earned a median annual salary of $73,300 in 2019, while advance practice nurses brought in median annual earnings of $115,800. BLS projects an increase in employment in the healthcare sector by 14 percent from 2018–2028. These salaries will vary and depend upon which part of the country you live in, what specialty you work in, and your years of experience. Coastal states usually have higher starting salaries than mid-western states do. Anecdotally, I know many registered nurses here in Los Angeles that work in specialty areas who bring in $140,000/year without ever working overtime. These nurses have decades of experience in their respective specialties and are experts in their field. Is that a realistic expectation if you have one year of experience and are living in central Florida? Most definitely not. Money should not be the sole driving factor to go into the nursing profession, but of course, it is a factor that must be considered in your educational investment.

University/College Accreditation

Researching the cost of your education is extremely important but equally important is the school's accrediting body. You do not want to go through all of the effort and expense to graduate from a program that is not accredited. The topic of accreditation can become very dicey depending upon your Board of Registered Nursing (BRN) and what state you live in. This is especially tricky because in today's online environment, many students are opting to enroll in programs that are not in their home state. This is largely due to the increased competitiveness of being accepted to a local school. You must always start by going to your BRN website and seeing which programs they have approved. The purpose of this is to ensure the program comprehensively covers knowledge that is essential, which ultimately serves to protect the public.

Another consideration is whether your individual program is either regionally or nationally accredited. Let's say that you started out in a Board-approved associate program that was regionally accredited. You graduated, passed the NCLEX-RN, and decided to do your RN to BSN. The BSN program you chose was nationally accredited, not regionally. You complete that program and decide to move on to your master's degree. What you did not consider is that many graduate programs will not accept a degree from a nationally accredited school. You will have to do exhaustive homework to find a school that will accept you into their graduate program. The point is you must do your due diligence with regard to researching school accreditation and make sure the accreditation aligns with what your future goals are. Are you planning on stopping with your BSN? If you are, then you are fine. Do you want to pursue academia and obtain a doctorate? If you do, then accreditation will play an even greater role in your continued education.

Regional and national accreditation applies not only to nursing degrees but all degrees in general. To further examine the importance of accreditation for nursing programs, you must also consider the Accreditation Commission for Education in Nursing (ACEN) and the Commission on Collegiate Nursing Education (CCNE). These accreditations are absolutely essential for any BSN program. Your BSN program must have these specific nursing accreditations regardless of what kind of regional or national accreditation is involved. You must be aware that non-accredited universities are a huge red flag and should be avoided. Accreditation is essential to federal financial aid, the acceptance of transfer credits, job market competitiveness, and as I stated, attending a graduate program. Do the homework now of researching your school's accreditation and save yourself from being stressed out later on. You must always keep in mind that any organization that advertises "become a nurse fast" is lying to you. There is no fast and easy way to become a registered nurse. That is why you need to fill your toolbox now with the knowledge to help you make an informed decision. You need to know who you are and what you want. Be aware of the importance of accreditation and board approval as it relates to your program choice.

CHAPTER 1 KEY POINTS:

- **What program best suits me? ADN/BSN/MSN**

- **Realistically, how long will my program take?**

- **How will I balance this program with work, family, etc. and be successful?**

- **How much is this going to cost, how am I going to pay for it?**

- **Calculate return on investment: consider the cost of education as it relates to earnings**

- **Is my program Board approved?**

- **Is my program accredited?**

- What type of accreditation does my college/university have?

- How does the type of accreditation impact my future educational endeavors/goals?

- Does my current employer provide reimbursement for this school?

- Does my program qualify for federal financial aid?

CHAPTER 2

Learn Everything You Can: In the End, You'll Still Know Nothing

Becoming a registered nurse means learning in perpetuity. It never ends, and that's exactly as it should be. We all couldn't wait to graduate from our program and start working and stop the relentless studying. Yes, as nursing students, we had to study a lot. There was about a fifty percent attrition rate in our school, which meant if you didn't do the work, you were quickly eliminated, and it's only gotten more competitive today. The work at times was grueling and all-consuming as we were expected to integrate all the didactic study and apply it to the clinical setting where you would encounter real human beings that were sick and experiencing probably the worst moments of their lives. Yup, this was stressful. But what is the point, you say? Well, the point being, through the perpetual pursuit of knowledge and the perpetual pursuit of clinical practice opportunities comes confidence and ultimately competence.

So, what do you do? Well, number one on the list is to get accepted to a program, then study hard and graduate. Study your butt off and then pass your NCLEX! Easy, right? Nope, I know it's not that easy, but that is the basic blueprint, and that, my friends, is just the beginning. And if you are already practicing as a newbie, just remember that this is just the very beginning of your journey. If you thought all the study was behind you, you will soon come to realize that in today's healthcare setting, you have just achieved the basics with the task of graduating and becoming licensed. Today's healthcare delivery system is more technologically complex than ever before, and while being a generalist on a medical-surgical unit was always an accepted entry into practice, it would better serve you to consider achieving advanced certifications prior to being accepted into a specialty area. To clarify, there are many specialized practice areas such as the Post Anesthesia Care Unit (PACU) that require certain clinical hours before being able to sit for a specialty certification exam. An example would be the Certified Post Anesthesia Nurse (CPAN) certification. A Certified Post Anesthesia certification requires many clinical practice hours within the PACU before being able to sit for the national exam. So, what would that mean for you? Well, not a whole lot because you would not be eligible to sit for this exam yet, but there are other routes to help you early in your career to achieve your goals. We will explore concepts to help you expedite your advancement to specialty areas of practice, but you will need to ask yourself some very specific questions relating to who you are, what you want, and where you want to be.

Nursing, as in medicine, has very broad practice areas and a never-ending body of collected scientific data that is constantly evolving. In today's job market, it is understood that the registered nurse must continue to study for advanced degrees as evidenced by the recommendations from organizations such as the Institute of Medicine, but that discussion is beyond the scope of this conversation. The intent of this book is to guide you with specific ideologies to help you attain confidence and competence within your chosen clinical specialty, as most registered nurses will start their professional practice as clinicians. With that being said, we will focus on concepts to help you attain an advanced entry point into clinical practice as a new nurse. As you climb your organization's clinical ladder, you may then wish to pursue other non-clinical opportunities as you progress toward academia.

Who Am I? Make Your Like List

This is a very basic question that I think we all ask of ourselves at one point or another, at some point in our lives, and not necessarily after a heavy night of drinking. Oh, I know, you don't drink, right? Anyway, know yourself. Know what patient populations you would like to work with and why. Are you very detail-oriented and like a certain level of control and predictability (Intensive Care Unit)? Do you thrive on adrenaline and unpredictability (Emergency Room)? Work to remain unbiased but develop a strong point of view and consider your innate abilities, quirks, or whatever you consider your strengths and how you would apply these qualities to a clinical practice setting to achieve positive outcomes. Also, explore what you consider your weaknesses and take on the painful task of exercising those "weak muscles" until you effect the change that you desire within yourself. Make a list. Examine what excites you or repels you. I have known many nurses over the years, and most ended up in specialties that matched their personalities and their personal "likes." Make a *Like List*. I have known nurses and nursing students who have witnessed a chest being opened for an open-heart surgery and did not blink an eye. I have witnessed other medical professionals come into an operating room suite, gaze upon that same open chest, and pass out. All while the attending was screaming, "Do not faint into the field, faint in the opposite direction!" Yes, he really did instruct this person to faint in the opposite direction. Some of these same individuals that were not fazed by any amount of blood were repulsed by any kind of respiratory secretion! These individuals obviously did not end up in a medical/respiratory ICU. So, choose your body fluids wisely! Establish what your passion is. Discover your personality type and what that means regarding how you cope with stress. These are all basic concepts that people often ignore but are essential to help define what you want. Remember, our profession is just like life. In fact, it is life and death. It's never perfect but beautiful, unpredictable, and ever-changing. Add a big pinch of stress to the mix and there you have it. Always strive to know yourself.

START BUILDING YOUR TOOLBOX:
GET YOUR ACLS NOW

I define your "Toolbox" as a strong foundation of knowledge that will serve you in your professional practice. You should begin to accumulate certifications such as Advanced Cardiac Life Support (ACLS), even if you are not sure what specialty you desire to work in. I may have a lot of naysayers, but I believe it is to your benefit to obtain these certifications before even knowing what you want to be when you grow up. Unlike CPAN certification, Critical Care Registered Nurse (CCRN) certification, or Certified Gastroenterology Registered Nurse (CGRN) certification, you are eligible as a nursing student or a newly minted nurse to study and sit for the Advanced Cardiac Life Support (ACLS) certification exam. Old-school ideology would recommend the new nurse to start off their clinical practice on a medical-surgical unit for a minimum of one year before seeking to advance their clinical practice to specialty areas. I strongly disagree, and I'm definitely old school. There is nothing wrong with starting off your career on a medical-surgical unit. There are countless opportunities to develop a strong foundation of practice in such a setting, but if given the opportunity to layer your knowledge base with these certifications, why would you not do it. Many new nurses feel they are missing out on the basics of med-surg by going directly to a specialty. This is not true. It may be overwhelming as a student or a new nurse, but before you graduate or while you are early on in your career, it would be in your best interest to pass the ACLS exam. Every specialty outside of med-surg requires that you possess a minimum competency in being able to interpret cardiac rhythms. ACLS provides a solid foundation on the interpretation of these rhythms and treatment guidelines and protocols for abnormal rhythms. By completing ACLS alone you open yourself up to myriad opportunities in telemetry/step-down units where you will encounter more than enough med-surg experiences. If ACLS seems overwhelming to you as a student, to make it more doable, take it in concert with, or upon completion of your cardiology rotation. They will complement each other. Upon completion of your ACLS, you will want to enroll in a 12-lead EKG interpretation course. This holds true for both the student and the novice nurse. 12-lead EKG interpretation will enhance what you've learned in ACLS. Your goal would be to complete these courses before your graduation. In this competitive market, recruiters are trained to look for these extra certifications when reviewing resumes from prospective employees. By having attained these certifications early on, you have set yourself apart from the pack.

WHAT ABOUT PALS?

PALS stands for Pediatric Advanced Life Support. As if ACLS wasn't challenging enough wait until you pursue this course. PALS is another valuable certification that you are eligible to obtain if you have enough motivation. Just as with ACLS, not only will you need to engage in the didactic portion of the curriculum, but you will need to be proficient in the "Mega-Codes." You will develop a strong foundation of knowledge and then will need to translate that knowledge into clinical practice scenarios orchestrated by your instructors, culminating in the Mega-Code. In this scenario, after you have enough understanding of the course material as evidenced by passing the American Heart Association (AHA) examination, you will proceed to be a team member and then ultimately a team captain and direct emergent care according to AHA guidelines and established protocols. For these courses, your instructors are usually emergency medicine doctors, nurses, and paramedics, all possessing extensive real-world emergency experience in the field and hospital settings. Upon completion of the AHA testing and successful performance in the Mega-Code, you will be certified for a period of two years. You must renew every two years and go through the entire process again while incorporating possible changes as evidenced by new science and practice guidelines. You should always be certified through the American Heart Association as certifications from other organizations are not recognized by many employers.

To ICU or Not ICU: The Debate Never Ends

Again, you may hear the guffaws of many naysayers on the distant horizon. Well, just ignore that and go directly to ICU if you can get the opportunity. Currently, many organizations offer what they call a Versant Residency Program, which is a comprehensive educational and training system for RN residents. This residency helps to transition new nurses into the highly complex hospital setting. These programs for new nurses run anywhere from six months to one year, and many programs and organizations offer new nurses the opportunity to start their careers in highly desirable specialty areas such as the ICU. Once the new nurse has been acclimated to this critical practice environment, he or she will have countless opportunities to transition into other specialty practice areas. Critical care is the basis and foundation for everything in the acute care hospital environment. One year of professional practice in the ICU will open doors for you. Never say no to this opportunity.

I have mentioned studying for your ACLS and PALS, which is a base of knowledge needed in the ICU setting. If you are not able to get a residency in the ICU setting, then it would behoove you to take an Advanced Hemodynamic Monitoring course. This curriculum will go further than ACLS and PALS and will explore concepts of hemodynamic monitoring with arterial lines and Swan-Ganz catheters. This is an essential foundation of knowledge that the ICU/specialty nurse must possess. If you cannot obtain the residency, then find this class. It will show prospective employers your aptitude, motivation, and dedication to increasing your knowledge base. This will create opportunities for you in the future.

Is Your Toolbox Full Yet?

Okay, you are well on the road to building a strong foundation of knowledge for your professional practice, your "toolbox" if you will. Do some of these recommendations sound a little overzealous? Sound possibly a little stressful to pursue?

I know, just graduating and passing the NCLEX examination alone is a major accomplishment, but in today's competitive market, you will need to incorporate more into your toolbox to stand out in an ocean of competitors. The hospital is a coveted job. Many newly minted registered nurses have found in today's current market that even having obtained advanced degrees, they cannot obtain hospital employment. Obviously, any opportunity for employment is a good thing, especially when just starting out in your career. But if you take employment outside of the hospital setting as your first job, it will be almost impossible to enter the hospital setting later on. That is why it is of utmost importance to try and obtain as many certifications and specialized training courses as possible. This not only will serve to make you more marketable but will also serve to help you know who you are and what you want. What could be more important than that?

Okay, Deep Breath and Put It in Perspective

So, you are the motivated type. You have an incredible thirst for learning, which you will need in this profession. And if you don't have an incredible thirst for learning, well, then you will be led to drink whether you like it or not. You do not take no for an answer and failure is not an option for you. You were a straight-A student and graduated with high honors. The computer shut down after only answering sixty questions on the NCLEX examination! You received your ACLS certification before you even graduated nursing school, and you are a whiz at 12-lead EKG interpretation. You aced your

Advanced Hemodynamic Monitoring curriculum and know all your pulmonary artery catheter waveforms and values by heart. You can shoot a cardiac output with your eyes closed and know what the systemic vascular resistance and cardiac index are just by listening to your patient breathe. LOL! Blood gas interpretation and the oxygen-hemoglobin dissociation curve are no brainers for you! Guess what? You still DON'T KNOW ANYTHING. Always keep that in mind because it's true. In the greater context of the vast amount of accumulated scientific knowledge in the modern world, you have only acquired an infinitesimal portion of it. You will need to dedicate yourself to become a lifelong learner as a registered nurse. You will never know all the answers no matter how smart you are, but you will need to know how to find those answers. Don't be afraid to ask questions. Don't be afraid to confer with colleagues. You don't know what you don't know. Even when you have acquired a vast amount of theoretical knowledge, you will then need to start your journey on integrating that knowledge into clinical practice. Here's where the fun begins. Let me help you put it in perspective. According to Benner (1982), there are five distinct levels of nursing experience, which include the novice, advanced beginner, competent, proficient, then finally, the expert status. The first of which is the novice, a beginner with no experience and who functions on a "rules-based" system without any critical thinking. (Don't be rigid in the protocols you've learned, ask questions, and don't blindly follow orders.) Then the clinician moves to advanced beginner status, having achieved some experiences in clinical scenarios which helps the individual to formulate a guide for action. Finally, we reach competent status. The nurse would need to complete a full two to three years of full-time clinical practice in the same practice environment, day in and day out, to achieve a designation of being competent! You are highly encouraged to obtain as much knowledge as possible in your formative years, but you will need day-to-day clinical experiences to solidify and incorporate this knowledge into competent practice. So, don't sweat it, and don't beat yourself up too badly because it's gonna take you years of practice to get where you wanna go. You'll get there. When you do, you will be a force to be reckoned with because you filled up your toolbox early on.

Chapter 2 Key Points:

- Devote 100 percent to your studies
  and learn everything you can.

- It's OK to acknowledge that you don't know
  everything (We know that, even if you don't).

- You don't know what you don't know,
  so please ask a million questions.

- Make your *Like List* to help you choose your specialty.

- Conversely acknowledge what you
  absolutely *do not like*.

- Don't know where you want to be? Take ACLS/PALS.

- Do know where you want to be. Take ACLS/PALS.

- If you can get an opportunity for residency in ICU/PACU/ER, then DO IT!

- Whatever specialty you choose, start logging your clinical hours and sit for certification.

- Evaluate what's in your toolbox besides your degree. What sets you apart?

CHAPTER 3

Don't Blindly Follow Orders: You Are Responsible for the Consequences

We are talking about clear, concise, effective communication among interdisciplinary team members here. Not mutiny on the bounty. We are not talking about refusing to execute an order just because you don't feel like doing it. What we are talking about is safe and effective communication. Collaboration, collegiality, and mutual professional respect, eh? Well, if there is none of that in your organization, then it would just come down to good old-fashioned CYA! As a nurse, you are legally bound to follow doctor's orders, so therein lies the rub. What if the attending surgical resident orders Ancef two grams intravenously on call to the operating room and your patient has a penicillin allergy? It is documented on the chart, and the patient states that he has an anaphylactic reaction to penicillin drugs. Well, you as the nurse know that there is approximately a 10 percent cross-sensitivity between penicillin and cephalosporins, and there is a very real risk that the patient may have an adverse reaction. If you didn't know that, well, that is an entirely different issue. But since you understand there is cross-reactivity between those classes of drugs, what would you do? Firstly, don't give that drug! I know, I know, it's a full surgery schedule today and your patient is the first case, and you don't want to delay the surgeon and the operating room. Your patient and his family are extremely anxious, your resident is extremely anxious, and now you are extremely anxious. You haven't even started your IV line and the anesthesiologist is trying to roll the patient into the room before you have even finished your medication reconciliation.

This scenario is very typical and happens all day and every day. This is but one very simple example in one very specific practice setting but is applicable to all settings. Back to the point of "learn everything you can 'cause in the end, you still know nothing." How does that help you? you ask. How I want it to help you is to impress upon you that you must always come from a place of knowing your role, and as a registered nurse, you will have many. But first and foremost, remember that you are an advocate for your patient. You are your patient's voice when he cannot advocate for himself. There are millions of drugs on the market, and you just can't memorize all of them. In today's healthcare setting, there are technological advancements to promote the safety of medication administration such as the use of scanners that have decreased medication errors. But that's not the point. The point is you as the RN knew this order from the resident was wrong. It is your duty to always question orders. You must always ask "why." You must understand the rationales behind what you are doing. As I have mentioned before, studying algorithms and protocols and becoming certified is wonderful and will serve to advance you in your chosen practice areas, but rote learning is no substitute for critical thinking. Just as was noted earlier, it takes about two to three years of daily clinical professional practice to become competent, to become "aware," if you will. It's like developing consciousness through years of varied clinical situations like the one that was just presented. You take all of that rote learning that we spoke of earlier and through those first few years of practice, you will develop your "soul." Remember, you will never know all the answers. Just ask, and practice asking a lot so you know where to find those answers.

THE LEGALITY OF FOLLOWING ORDERS: KNOW YOUR SCOPE

In whatever state or states you will work, know your scope of practice. The Nurse Practice Act (NPA) is a statute enacted by the legislature, which delineates the legal scope of practice of nursing within its jurisdiction. This is content that is not covered in school, at least not when I attended, but it is important to be aware of not only your scope but the scope of other licensed and ancillary personnel as you will be delegating tasks to these individuals. Of course, you also need to be familiar with your organization's policy and procedures regarding your scope of practice. You will need to be confident with this knowledge as other licensed medical personnel may, believe it or not, have no clue as to what your scope is. This can be particularly tricky if you are working in specialty areas such as interventional radiology, special procedures, PACU, interventional endoscopy, etc., and are working with residents, especially residents.

So, you are very motivated and have a relentless thirst for learning and took some humble guidance from this book and got that Versant Residency in ICU. You were accepted straight out of school and into the Medical Intensive Care Unit. You completed a very successful two years of service in the ICU and developed a very specialized critical care skill set. You have decided that you would like to transfer into a procedural area. This is something that always interested you from your clinical rotations in school. Again, as emphasized earlier, usually the only route to getting into a specialty procedure area is by having ICU experience. And you got it! You interview for an interventional radiology position. You blow them away, and you get the job. You complete a successful orientation. On the first day off of orientation, there were only a few IR cases, so you were floated to the main PACU. They have many surgical cases today, and the patient acuity levels are extremely high, and there are many complex surgeries on the schedule. The PACU staff is extremely happy to have you float to them because they are perpetually short-staffed. They know your ICU background, so they are confident you will catch on to the PACU routine quickly. The PACU charge nurse knows you are not used to the PACU routine, so he has assigned you a thoracic case that has been in surgery for about six hours. The operating room is calling out for a bay to admit the patient. You're up! The anesthesiologist gives you a bedside report. The patient has multiple chest tubes, a radial arterial line, and is still intubated. After zeroing your arterial line, you notice that the cuff pressure matches the A-line. The patient has a 95 mm hg systolic blood pressure. The anesthesiologist states that this is within the patient's baseline blood pressure. There are currently no vasopressors being titrated at this time. Before you even complete your post-anesthesia/post-surgical assessment of your patient, a very hurried young guy in a white coat with a stethoscope around his neck walks in and states, "I need to do a fiberoptic bronchoscopy on this patient now!" You look over at the charge nurse as he's making other assignments; he glances at you and nods his head and yells, "Yeah, I'll be right there to help you." What does that mean? You ask to see the doctor's badge; he identifies himself as Dr. Whoever, the Fellow. Anyway, you confirm this is really Dr. Whoever. You confirm that he has privileges to do what he states he needs to do. You even confirm with the attending that Dr. Whoever wants to do this "right now!" and query if this is even indicated at this moment post-surgery in the PACU. You ask and confirm, and confirm, and confirm. Greenlight. It's a go. As you are monitoring the patient, Dr. Whoever is profusely sweating and appears very rushed. He looks more tachycardic than the patient. In that moment, Dr. Whoever tells you to draw up a syringe of propofol. You know, Michael Jackson juice. Got milk? You use a 10 ml syringe to draw up the milky white stuff. The syringe now contains 10 mg/ml of propofol. You hand him the syringe.

He looks at you like you are crazy and hands it back to you. He states, "*I'm* gonna bronch the patient, and *you're* gonna sedate him, I'll tell you when to give it, I want you to give 10 mg at a time." Well, what do you do, Mr. ICU? You have a critical care background, have initiated, maintained, and titrated countless propofol drips, high dose ketamine drips, and fentanyl drips among myriad other titratable drugs. You are certified to give moderate sedation. You are comfortable sedating patients with fentanyl and versed while maintaining their airway, so what do you do? Well, it comes down to don't just blindly follow orders, even if you're technically comfortable executing those orders. Propofol is a widely utilized anesthetic agent. It falls under the domain of anesthesia. There are currently warnings on the propofol label that state only clinicians that are trained in the administration of general anesthesia should use this drug. Technically, even a cardiologist shouldn't be administering this drug to a patient. When was the last time you administered general anesthesia? It is interesting to note that there is data to support the use of propofol by adequately trained non-anesthesiologist providers. The American College of Gastroenterology is currently lobbying state regulatory boards to accept nurse-administered propofol sedation for their endoscopic procedures. Of course, certified registered nurse anesthetists can function in this capacity. But they have a different scope of practice. In this scenario, you would call your CRNA or anesthesiologist, but do not practice outside of your scope even though Dr. Whoever wants you to do it.

Chapter 3 Key Point:

- Know your scope! Review your state Board of Registered Nursing website and review your board's Scope of Practice document.

CHAPTER 4

Work Environment: Hi Ho! Off to Work We Go!

Most nurses want to begin their career in the coveted hospital setting. Most RN students do their clinical rotations only in the hospital setting. Just like a nurse is a nurse is a nurse (not!), a hospital is a hospital is a hospital just does not hold true. There are many different types of hospital organizations. There are different levels of trauma centers all designating different levels of service that may be available for very specific patient populations. There are for-profit versus nonprofit organizations, there are community hospitals, urban and rural hospitals, trauma centers, and union versus non-union hospitals. There is the Magnet-designated hospital along with the Pathway to Excellence certified organization. This brings us back to the concept of knowing who you are and defining what you want so that you may identify the most desirable place you want to work in. Obviously, if you are graduating and attempting to grab your first job, you may not have the bargaining power that you might wish. This is why it is important to have been driven to go the extra mile and obtain the certifications that were mentioned previously. You want to have as much of a competitive edge as possible when vying for a new position. There is huge competition to get into a Versant Residency Program, and you need to be prepared to have a step-up on your competitors.

Profit versus Non-Profit

There are many great organizations that are classified as either for-profit or nonprofit. Generally, according to the internal revenue service, nonprofit hospitals are classified as charities under the tax code. In exchange for not being required to pay federal income tax, nonprofits are expected to contribute funds via health and wellness programs to the surrounding communities. For-profit hospitals are privately owned companies. These companies are driven to make profits for their shareholders. It has been noted that for-profit hospital chains such as Tenet Healthcare are considered to be the highest billing hospitals in the country. You may or may not notice a difference in the daily operations of these organizations, but as a nurse on the frontlines, you may be able to discern certain nuances. Every organization, whether for-profit or nonprofit, must sustain financial viability in order to engage in daily business. Non-profits tend to furnish more uncompensated care whereas for-profits tend to suffer heavy financial burdens when caring for the uninsured. Depending on the company, as a nurse, you may encounter organizations that just do not have the budget to maintain equipment, electronic medical record systems, or the physical structure itself. I worked for a small for-profit hospital for many years, and although their rate of compensation was greater or equal to their competitors in the community, they were unable to maintain the basic physical structures of the building. I worked in the operating room, which was located in the basement. We had one patient elevator next to the operating room that we used to transport patients to the floor or ICU after surgery. This elevator was dedicated to serving patients only. No public access whatsoever. One day the elevator broke, and five years later, it was still broke. We had to use the only other common public elevator to transport our patients. Sometimes we needed to use this public elevator to bring patients to the morgue. Uncomfortable, to say the least. Imagine being in that public elevator with your postmortem care patient in his white body bag and then transferring your patient out of that public elevator that opened to the general hospital admissions desk. When you took the long way to the morgue, you got to engage in a meet and greet with the public. "Mommy, mommy, I wanna see what's in that big white bag!" Yup, this was a workflow concern for us all. We were told our broken patient transport elevator could not be fixed because it wasn't in the budget. The administration stated that because of logistical issues there would never be a budget to repair this transport elevator. These are anecdotal observations, but in reality, there are very real workflow issues that you may encounter related to the hospital's financial health.

Trauma Center versus Community Hospital

Academic Medical Centers (AMC) or Teaching Hospitals offer an expansive range of medical services from basic care to very complex care. AMCs deliver a disproportionate amount of care to specific populations which include Medicare and Medicaid recipients, trauma patients, and transfer patients from other facilities that require complex services. AMCs are instrumental in scientific research and have contributed to medical breakthroughs throughout history. Currently, the local AMC that I work for is engaged in developing new and innovative antibiotic therapies that utilize ultraviolet light.

Community Medical Centers are non-academic providers; they do not provide a venue for medical education and do not receive federal funds for research initiatives. Local community hospitals are excellent in providing basic care services to their neighborhood populations. Some community hospitals may not offer specialized services such as obstetrics, labor and delivery, neonatal care, or cardiac catheterization services.

Union versus Non-Union

What part of the country you live in will determine the prevalence of union versus non-union organizations. Places such as Florida are considered "right-to-work" states and generally do not have many organized labor unions. In a non-union organization, labor, and yes, you will find out that as a licensed medical professional, you are considered labor, will function at the sole discretion of the hospital management. Well, "What is so bad about that?" you might ask. The answer is nothing, but you should keep in mind when dealing with a work-related issue that there is no mediating body that will represent you. In a non-union environment, salary is calculated in many ways including years of experience, market price, and specialty. Maintaining your job will be largely dependent upon performance and excelling at climbing a clinical ladder, especially if it is a Magnet hospital. There is usually some kind of room for negotiating your salary.

In unionized environments, which are more prevalent in California, you will have a union representative that would guide you in any mediation process that may be related to work issues. Labor representatives in unionized environments seek to negotiate nurse salaries, retirement benefits, working conditions, and patient safety issues. Nurse labor contracts are negotiated with the hospital administrators and union representatives, and these contracts may extend over a period of years. When you are employed in a "union house," your hiring salary and benefits package are determined by these negotiated contracts, so largely you cannot haggle with human resources for a greater salary or other perks. Your salary will be based on a years of experience grid. You must also be aware that you will pay union dues. Usually, these dues are calculated based upon your employment status, full-time versus part-time, etc. These dues are subtracted bi-weekly. Unionization poses unique issues in the healthcare industry because oftentimes, when contracts end, the way to bargain for increased wages, benefits, and patient safety concerns is to strike. A strike is a work stoppage that may be disruptive to patient care activities.

You will need to choose which environment may prove to be most beneficial for you. At first, you may not have a choice in which environment you will work, but be aware of these distinctions and what resources you have at your hands to advocate for your clients and yourself.

MAGNET DESIGNATION: WHAT IS IT?

The Magnet Recognition Program elevates patient care while elevating the professional nurse's practice. The professional nurse collaborates with the interprofessional team and is instrumental in leadership and the dissemination and utilization of new scientific knowledge. The American Nurses Credentialing Center's Magnet Recognition Program designates certain worthy organizations worldwide, whose leaders demonstrate the ability to utilize the Magnet Model to effect superior patient outcomes, with Magnet status. Well, what does all that mean? Basically, a hospital must make an application to the American Nurses Credentialing Center's Magnet Program. The hospital will jump through huge hoops to satisfy the specific criteria that have been demonstrated to prove positive patient outcomes through professional nursing actions that have been empirically measured. Magnet concepts are designed to effect the reformation of healthcare, the discipline of nursing, and care of patient, family, and community (American Nurses Association [ANA], 2015). This is no easy task for a hospital to achieve. It can take a hospital years to achieve Magnet status, and it has been estimated that the cost to achieve Magnet status for an organization comes with a price tag of $2,000,000.00. It is estimated that only 6–8 percent of hospitals in the United States have achieved Magnet Status ("Magnet Model," n.d.). So, does that sound like the kind of organization you would like to work for? Oh, I know. Any job would be good right now, but it might be in your best interest professionally to gain employment in a Magnet-designated hospital. I believe that as you start off your career, at some point you should aim to seek employment in a Magnet-designated organization. It definitely won't be a punching a clock then forget about it when you go home kind of job. You will be immersed in a culture of progress. You will be expected to grow professionally in ways that go beyond your direct patient care. You will be expected to be a leader even at a very low-level clinical ladder designation. You will be groomed to think outside of the box. You will not just take orders from a physician; you will formally collaborate with a group of physicians through monthly committees regarding specific patient issues in your department. You will identify workflow problems, patient care issues, and identify technological innovation that will serve to effect positive patient outcomes. Guess what? Once you identify those problems, you will be expected to collect data, generate data, and analyze and synthesize the data. Once you've done that, you will be expected to present this information to your nurse and physician colleagues and petition for new evidence-based protocols that will improve patient outcomes on your unit, all through *your* initiatives. Oh, and yes, all of that is in addition to taking care of the 60 scheduled surgical patients for today!

PATHWAY TO EXCELLENCE PROGRAM

Similar to the Magnet Program, the American Nurses Credentialing Center has also created the Pathway to Excellence Program, which recognizes organizations that consistently adhere to the Pathway's structure and process which promotes healthy work environments (ANA, 2015). What does that mean to you as a nurse? It means that if you seek employment in this kind of organization, you will work in an environment that promotes nurse autonomy and control of practice. This kind of program creates an environment that emphasizes worker safety and addresses patient care and practice issues. The nurse is given a voice and is encouraged to be heard when it comes to work and patient safety issues. An organization that is dedicated to following the structure of a Pathway to Excellence Program seeks to provide professional development for the nurse, ensure equitable compensation, and recognizes that the work-life balance of the nurse is paramount to positive outcomes for both staff and patient.

Just as an employer will examine what you have to offer, you need to be able to analyze and examine the structure and culture of the organization that you desire to work for. Understanding the structure of the organization will give you insight into the organization's culture. Is the organization vested in your professional development? Does the structure and culture of the organization lend to frontline staff having a voice? These factors will largely determine your day-to-day professional work experience. Whatever environment you choose to work in, and no matter how difficult to navigate your way through it in the beginning, you must always remember your allegiance to your status as an independently licensed professional. Know your state's Nurse Practice Act as well as your board's position on your scope of practice. Know the scope of other colleagues and providers. Know the scope of other personnel that you will delegate to. Develop your advocacy skills and maintain your clinical competency and you will do well. Practice beneficence, nonmaleficence, justice, fidelity, and veracity, and you will succeed in any environment.

CHAPTER 4 KEY POINTS:

- Identify the type of organization you are pursuing

- Is the organization for-profit or nonprofit?

- Is the organization unionized or non-unionized?

- Is the organization a community hospital or a trauma center?

- Is the organization a Magnet hospital?

- If not Magnet, is the organization actively pursuing Magnet status?

- What are the staffing laws or policies of the state you will work in?

- All of these factors will affect your salary negotiation

- All of these factors will determine your career advancement

- All of these factors will determine your work-life balance

- All of these factors will determine your career satisfaction

CHAPTER 5

Why Do Nurses Eat
Their Young? Yum!

The nursing profession is a helping profession, but what you may discover in your clinical rotations or in your professional practice, is the age-old dilemma of the senior nurse's desire to eat you up and spit you out. Now, that sounds absolutely horrible, right? Counterintuitive to what we represent as a profession. Nursing is by and large an altruistic profession. That in and of itself has subjected our profession to a lack of advocacy for ourselves. We, as nurses, have given our skills, heart, soul, and dedication to the promotion of healing and meeting the needs of others. I must add, meeting the needs of others without regard for taking care of ourselves. We do this daily for years and for decades, relentlessly advocating tirelessly (until we get very tired) for the very complex needs of others. This, my friends, is the crux of many issues that ail us as a profession.

Obviously, you are discovering, or may have already discovered, that the profession of nursing is extremely stressful and competitive. Just like any other profession, there are toxic situations, circumstances, and people. Our work stress is highlighted by the fact that in our profession, it is our duty to engage head-on into the stress of our patients and families. We don't run or avoid those situations; it is our duty to willingly participate in them, to be present for some of the worst situations that humanity faces. The competitiveness of our intense training and the nature of our job has the potential to breed toxic scenarios when dealing with our colleagues. It is essential to have a basic understanding of why another professional would want to undermine you or your potential. Not only has nursing school become increasingly competitive but the modern work environment of the nurse has also become more difficult to navigate than at any other time in our history.

LATERAL/HORIZONTAL VIOLENCE

Christie and Jones (2014) define lateral violence as harmful behavior in the workplace perpetrated by one employee against another. This phenomenon is very common and devastating in the nursing workforce. Lateral violence is synonymous with "bullying" and is characterized by inappropriate or disruptive behavior in the work environment by one employee to the other who may hold equal status or a lesser position in the organization. The negative impact of lateral violence is significant. It has tremendous harmful effects upon the nurse and may impair the nurse's ability to deliver optimal care to the patient. Lateral violence is insidious in nature. It may not be one isolated incident but rather an ongoing and subtle barrage of nonphysical micro-aggressive behaviors. These individual acts are manifested through ongoing personalized insults over time, which may cause great damage and harm to the recipient. Unfortunately, the nursing profession has been identified as the occupation most at risk for lateral violence. It is estimated that 44–85 percent of nurses have been victims of lateral violence, while an astounding 93 percent of nurses have reported witnessing lateral violence in the workplace (Christie & Jones, 2014). It has been documented that, commonly, the experienced nurse has been identified as the perpetrator of this abuse. Nursing students and novice nurses are often subjected to lateral violence. The lateral violence phenomenon is so prevalent in the nurse's work environment that many unit cultures have normalized this damaging practice. Consequently, by normalizing this dysfunctional culture of abuse, there is an absence of reporting this deleterious behavior. It is a vicious cycle of abuse. Christie and Jones (2014) note that victims of lateral violence report a negative world view, poor self-esteem, ineffective coping strategies, and psychological stress disorders. It is noted that lateral violence is often perpetrated by nurse managers and directors, which makes it even more difficult for the nurse to report the behavior. This phenomenon must be addressed as it impacts an organization's ability to provide a venue for safe and effective care to their clients. There is a huge financial impact to the organization related to nurse attrition and onboarding new employees. Many studies have reported that the levels of stress and burnout in nursing are higher than among members of the armed forces (Christie & Jones, 2014). The stress of the job compounded with the individual stressors of home and family life only exacerbate this problem. People become the "walking wounded" and report to work needing an outlet to vent their own personal frustrations. That venting of negative emotions usually is thrust upon vulnerable peers. It is noted that the most common targets of lateral violence are new graduates, but lateral violence is perpetrated at all levels.

DEAR INSTRUCTOR: PLEASE DON'T BULLY ME, OK?

This cycle of bullying likely starts in nursing school. Many instructors feel an air of superiority in their curriculum and sometimes feel dedicated to "weeding people out" of the program. This is unfortunate but many times true. Sometimes instructors feel like they are doing you no favors by hand-holding. This is a tough profession, so they begin to indoctrinate you into what they perceive to be the "realities" of the profession. Anecdotally, I recall an instructor that I thought just couldn't stand me. As you have, I worked, studied, and prepared rigorously for all my clinical rotations but was filled with dread every time I would engage with this certain instructor. When drawing up medication, my hands would literally shake as I perceived she gazed upon me with contempt. She not only verbally condemned my performance but was an expert at expressing her contempt for me with nonverbal cues. When I would ask a question that I felt was appropriate prior to medication administration, I would receive her famous "eye roll." Her notorious rolling of the eyes at me followed by a twitch in the left upper eyelid left me feeling a lack of self-confidence, to say the least. These are classic signs of bullying (twitch excepted), and I was experiencing it well before I would ever work professionally. I was fortunate to innately develop some coping skills with this particular individual because honestly, your instructors have literal power over your success and subsequently your future! Talk about stress. I got through that clinical rotation and did not experience another clinical instructor that was as dedicated to busting my...well, you know what I mean.

Organizations, like people, have specific cultures and personalities. As I have discussed previously, your work environment will dictate your work happiness and professional growth. Some units in some organizations have "clique cultures." Just like high school. It is always difficult to be the new kid on the block. But when you are the new kid entering a unit with the culture of eating their young, you better have some tools in that "toolbox" we talked about. Believe it or not, sometimes very experienced nurses can be threatened by someone half their age coming into "their" practice setting. As referenced before, there is absolutely no substitute for clinical experience, but even with all the experience in the world, some seasoned nurses are threatened and defensive and are not open to mentoring new nurses. I have witnessed a brand-new nurse with less than a year of clinical experience (already achieved a master's degree) be chastised openly by a seasoned nurse for her lack of knowledge regarding a procedure. This seasoned nurse was formally chosen by the administration to be this new nurse's preceptor. When the new nurse's formal preceptor was not at work, I was informed that I would take the role of the preceptor in her absence. I found the orientee to be extremely bright, willing to take constructive criticism, and open to discussing rationales for doing something (remember evidence-based practice). I recognized that even being master's prepared, she would need to log many hours of clinical experience to fully integrate her formal education into practice and become competent. She just needed time, support, guidance, and patience. For whatever personal reason, her bully preceptor could not provide her with that support. I learned that after close to one year of practice in that unit, the new nurse filed for stress leave and then never returned. This individual was only in her twenties and just beginning her career. Pretty lousy way to start, I think. I believe the culture of the leadership, which often reflects the culture of the organization, had a lot to do with this individual's untimely exodus. To be honest, the "clique culture" of that unit was to eat not only their young but anyone they could sink their teeth into.

The ANA (2015) cites the National Institute for Occupational Safety and Health as reporting that healthcare workers are at an increased risk of experiencing workplace violence when compared to the overall workforce. This is important to note as bullying and workplace hostility have a significant impact not only on the nurse but contribute to poor patient outcomes as well. Nurses need to become advocates to nurses as well as their patients. Advocate for yourself first. As we have discussed earlier, take the time to get to know who you are. How do you respond to conflict? What is your communication style? What kind of personality types trigger you? It is essential to recognize your own biases. It is essential to recognize how you give criticism as well as how you receive it. You will not be able to control other people's inappropriate behavior in your work environment. You will only be able to control how you receive and react to this kind of behavior. That is not to say to be passive and just accept bullying. Many times, the bully will seek out "victims" based upon the perception of the receiving individual's lack of ability to "fight back." Many students and new nurses feel like they don't have a voice and are relegated to just toughing it out when encountering a bully. There is a myriad of things in professional nursing practice that you will definitely have to tough out, but bullying is not one of them. Develop your ability to advocate for yourself and create your own well-being. Developing self-advocacy skills will only strengthen your ability to be someone else's advocate. You do not have to be silenced if you are being bullied. In fact, it is your duty to speak out. In an organization, hierarchical structures and perceived status may lend to bully culture. Modern professional nursing is based on interprofessional communication, collaboration, and collegiality. Regardless of your role and scope of practice, you are or will be a licensed professional. This is why I have earlier emphasized organizational structures and discussed programs such as Magnet that strive for collegial interprofessional collaboration and the promotion of positive work environments for the nurse. Without respectful communication and collaboration among interdisciplinary colleagues, there can only be a toxic workplace, fragmented care, and poor patient outcomes. Respectful communication is a must for safe and effective patient care. I can tell you, countless times I have witnessed a surgeon throw an instrument in anger across an operating room table. Throwing an instrument in anger across the operating room table during surgery is not good for the patient or anybody else for that matter, including the surgeon. This behavior is no longer tolerated in today's healthcare setting. Regardless of the organizational hierarchy and the emphasis on the surgeon's ability to generate income for the hospital, there are avenues to stop this behavior. Whether it's the surgeon or even the nursing assistant that is the perpetrator of abuse, this behavior must be stopped.

Options: Stopping the Bully Culture

The Joint Commission has established standards for leadership that mandate agencies to recognize and intervene to correct inappropriate and disruptive behaviors in the workplace. Your management must be engaged to identify lateral violence in its early stages. Your manager is responsible to identify individuals who are having difficulties managing their stress, as these individuals are likely to engage in the bullying of others. Referrals may be made to employee assistance programs (EAPs) to help individuals engage in stress reduction strategies. Staff members may also be engaged in reporting these individuals who consistently demonstrate bullying behaviors. A management team partnering with staff to identify toxic behaviors in the workplace will be the first step in mitigating the negative effects of this behavior. Successful strategies involve the entire unit team in building and promoting positive relationships with one another. Unfortunately, some unit cultures contain deeply engrained toxic behaviors and relationships that are difficult to change. If you are uncomfortable reporting lateral violence directly to your manager, many organizations provide anonymous hotlines to address these issues.

CHAPTER 5 KEY POINTS:

- **Define lateral/horizontal violence**
- **Identify the personality types and communication styles of colleagues in your environment**
- **What are some bullying behaviors?**
- **How do you respond to bullying?**
- **Do you directly address the bully's behavior?**
- **Do you ignore bullying?**
- **What are your resources on your unit/school if you feel bullied?**
- **Identify advocates or mentors in your environment**
- **Inventory your strengths/weaknesses in communicating your discomfort in a situation**

- What are your lateral violence reporting options in your organization?

- Do you have an anonymous hotline in your organization to report lateral violence?

CHAPTER 6

Nursing Is Art and Science
So, What's Art?

I love to frequently acknowledge that nursing is a great profession. Often, I have found myself describing this profession to others as an exemplary practice of artistry and science. Well, what does that mean? Personally, I don't think I understood the art of nursing until very recently, after logging in tens of thousands of clinical hours. Art in nursing can be interpreted in many ways and demonstrated to the person receiving nursing in many ways. The art of nursing embraces intangible assets. The ANA (2015) describes the art of nursing as based on caring and a respect for human dignity. This would embrace spirituality, healing, and compassion. The individual act of caring for another cannot be quantitatively measured. It is highly subjective and interpreted in different ways between the individual "delivering" care and the individual "receiving" the care. The ANA (2015) notes tenets of the *Human Caring Science Theory*, which emphasizes the relationship between the nurse and the patient and how this relationship is instrumental in assisting the patient to find meaning in illness, suffering, and pain. This is an existential dilemma we all face. The dilemma of being able to translate the nurse's scientific knowledge, training, and skills into something intangible, something that touches someone's soul. In order to facilitate this process, the professional nurse must develop professional maturity. How do you develop professional maturity? you may ask. By practicing for many years. This is why I referenced that I hadn't really been "woke" to the art of nursing until many years into practice. I recall an occasion during my first year on a step-down open-heart unit where unwittingly, I did not fully integrate the art of nursing in the care of one particular patient. Our patient population on the heart unit was very specific. These were very complex patients with high acuities. I had begun to rack up daily clinical experiences, specifically related to patients who had just received open-heart surgery. This patient population and this specific practice area were beginning to become my comfort zone. I was beginning to develop confidence with maintaining central venous catheters, chest tubes, mediastinal tubes, and epicardial atrial and ventricular pacing wires. I was confident with the maintenance of external digital pacemakers that were attached to the epicardial wires which came out of the patient's chest. The technical management of all of those tasks was becoming routine. I was confident in my practice, but I must admit, I was still overly consumed with the *technical* aspect of nursing. I was super functional in the execution of tasks, just like a robot. "Domo arigato, Nurse Roboto." Just google it. The focus on the technical aspect of my job could not have been overemphasized because the human being in front of me frequently had an absent underlying heart rhythm. Oftentimes, these patients were dependent on the external pacemakers to sustain their lives, so the technical knowledge and confidence of the nurse in monitoring these devices was essential. Anyway, I believe I was missing a lot of art in my practice because I was so focused on the technicalities. At the time, I was not cognizant of my lack of artistry until I had to take care of an overflow patient that was not a cardiac patient. Our cardiac patient population was being prepared to adapt to their new life after heart surgery. We were preparing these patients to transition to a healthy new life after surgery and ultimately discharge them home. The overflow patient I was assigned to take care of on this day was a cancer patient. Metastasis. A palliative care encounter. I do not recall how this assignment was made or the circumstances behind why this patient was brought to our unit, but I do recall the level of my discomfort at the time of being assigned to this patient. The patient was using a patient-controlled analgesia (PCA) pump. At the time, my default mode was to focus on the technical aspects of patient care, so I did just that. I did my best with the maintenance of the PCA, intravenous fluids, and focused on the management of the patient's pain. Instinctively, as a human being to another human being, I did my best to ensure the patient's comfort in this setting. Granted, the focus of my limited practice as a new nurse was on acute care, not hospice care. As I look back on that scenario, I realize I was woefully underprepared to practice the art of nursing for someone who was dying. I had based all of my nursing practice on the development of technical skills, not people skills. At the time, I did not realize it, but this palliative care experience would have an impact on how I would deliver the art of human caring to a personal situation.

FROM ROBOT TO HUMAN BEING

My grandmother, a diabetic, had largely been a noncompliant patient her whole life. Her noncompliance with her diabetes would lead to a limb being removed and other poor health outcomes. One day as I visited her in a nursing facility, I noticed she was tachypneic, a respiratory rate of 26–30 respirations per minute. She was using accessory muscles to breathe, and it took great effort for her to speak. I asked the nurse to bring me a pulse oximeter, and it read 88 percent on room air. This was not good. It was afternoon, and I speculated she must have been like this all morning. I asked the nurse to please notify the doctor right away of these assessment findings. A chest X-ray was ordered and indicated that she was in fluid overload. Her lungs were filling up with fluid fast. She was admitted to the hospital, intubated, and was brought to ICU. The next thing I recall was the attending MD telling me that my grandmother was in multisystem organ failure. Family discussions ensued. Decisions were made, and before you know it, I accompanied her from ICU to hospice. The whole process seemed way too fast and overwhelming to me, to say the least, and I worked in healthcare. It was late and family was present, but they all stated that they would visit in the morning. I said that I would like to remain by her side. I would sleep over. My grandmother's mind was completely intact. She was too weak to speak but would often glance over at me to see if I still remained by her side. I never left. The hospice nurse would come in and check on her every so often and give her a drop of sublingual morphine. It was now 3 a.m. We had just arrived at hospice the prior evening at 6 p.m. I was tired and emotionally drained. I held her hand. I rubbed her head. I spoke to her and let her know how much she was loved, and then I drifted off to sleep. At some point, I was awakened by the hospice nurse as she stated, "Robert, she is breathing about six respirations per minute now. It's gonna be soon." I thanked her for waking me up. I held my grand-mother's hand until her last breath. Just as she passed away, the phone rang. It was 5:20 a.m. It was my mother asking how she was doing. I can tell you that in those last moments of my grandmother's life, she did not care about what kind of degree I had. She did not care about all of my certifications. She did not care about all of my clinical experience or technical com-petency. In those last moments of her life, all she cared about was that I was present. Not just physically present but *present*. Present in the moment with her. There is a huge impact that you will make by being present, by holding a hand, by mak-ing eye contact, by giving a hug, or just by being in the same room. Be *present*.

In the beginning, I think we are all focused on becom-ing technically competent with the skills needed to function as a professional nurse. I want you to consider the first time you attempted an invasive procedure on a patient. Whether it be inserting a nasogastric tube, inserting a foley catheter, assisting with central venous line insertion, or 2,500 other procedures that you will develop competency with. The point being, until there is some mastery achieved with these skill sets, you will undoubtedly be more focused on the task at hand and with its safe execution, rather than focusing on the human being in front of you. We have all done it. Focusing on one piece of the puzzle rather than the entire complex picture. That's ok. It is essential to build confidence with your technical skills. You must be technically competent to deliver safe and effective care. But you must also remember that we are performing technical skills on human beings. Keep filling your toolbox with knowledge and build a mastery of technical skills. Before you know it, your toolbox will be close to full and then you will be able to practice the true, beautiful art of nursing. Always look for any opportunity, no matter how small, to incorporate the art of being human into your professional practice.

THIS IS SCIENCE

Professional nursing practice does not exist in a bubble of repetitively and mindlessly executing physician ordered tasks. Countless times I have witnessed laypersons attest to their understanding of what a nurse does as "following orders." I have had other nurse colleagues exclaim, "I just follow orders." Uh, hello! Mindlessly following orders will not only get you in trouble but your patient as well. I had an anesthesiologist yell across the room at me as he was running into another case. He exclaimed, "Did you see the order I wrote for that patient? Make sure it's appropriate for the patient, don't just give it and then chart that I told you to do it!" LOL. That statement from him would constitute a big "DUH!" So, if nurses don't just blindly follow orders, then what defines our practice and what is the basis for our critical thinking? The ANA (2015) notes that nurses function and base their critical decision-making processes on science. Nurses as practitioners of science utilize both qualitative and quantitative evidence to guide practice. Again, we will reference one scientific model, the nursing process, which includes assessment, diagnosis, outcome identification, planning, implementation, and evaluation (ANA, 2015). This process is a critical thinking framework and supports evidence-based practice. You should know that Florence Nightingale was a pioneer who advocated for the adoption and incorporation of nursing research into clinical practice. Nightingale created the basis for autonomous nursing practice that is distinct from medicine while still emphasizing the significance of collecting and using empirical evidence to drive nursing practice. The ANA (2015) describes evidence-based practice (EBP) as a problem-solving method that utilizes the best evidence from peer-reviewed research studies, clinical expertise, as well as evidence from the consumer's health history and condition. The EBP process assists clinicians to develop and formulate a testable question. The asking of a testable question as it relates to a patient-centered problem is the basis for this scientific framework. Peer-reviewed literature, critical appraisal of this literature, and synthesis of this information yield new science-based knowledge which can be translated into evidence-based practice that improves patient outcomes. This process is testable. Outcomes are measurable. Okay, is that clear? Let's break it down and make it more user friendly for you. Simple example. We talked about a testable question, so let's explore what that is. Say your unit serves a patient population seeking services related to the pancreas and biliary system. This patient population seeks advanced interventional endoscopy procedures such as endoscopic retrograde cholangiopancreatography (ERCP). You as the nurse service this population daily. You know as the nurse on this unit that there is an increased risk of post-ERCP pancreatitis after pancreatic duct dilation, contrast medium injected into the pancreas, multiple attempts to cannulate the papilla of Vater, and pancreatic sphincterotomy. You also know that those procedures are commonly done every day on these patients. Anecdotally, you notice in the PACU where you work that there has been an increase in the rate of admissions to the hospital after ERCP due to post-ERCP pancreatitis. You have not collected any data on this observation as of yet. You decide to engage a team and formulate a testable question as it relates to this problem you have observed: 1) Your question identifies a specific population of interest. (Pancreas and Biliary patients having an ERCP.) 2) Your question identifies an intervention based on peer-reviewed research. 3) Your question compares one intervention to another (Comparison of interest) 4) Your question examines the outcome. Ok, so what's the testable question? It looks like: *In patients with biliary disease (1. population), how does the use of nonsteroidal anti-inflammatory drugs*

(2. Intervention) compared to not utilizing nonsteroidal anti-inflammatory drugs either prophylactically or post procedurally (3. Comparison) affect the risk of developing post-ERCP pancreatitis (4. Outcome)? So, there you have it. You, as the nurse, through your clinical observations in your unit have decided to take action and create a team to examine a testable question that relates to your patient population. This project, depending upon measured outcomes for this question, may be the basis for the creation of new evidence-based practice guidelines in your unit that would decrease the incidence of post-ERCP pancreatitis. You are improving patient outcomes by your engagement in evidence-based practice! We have talked about interprofessional collaboration, and this project will necessitate that. You, as the nurse, will need to identify and engage department stakeholders to kickstart this project. When you have presented your testable question to involved stakeholders and your project has been approved, you will start the data collection process. You are on your way to helping in the creation of new evidence-based practice guidelines that will improve patient outcomes.

Chapter 6 Key Points:

- Understand that professional nursing is not based on task orientation

- Recognize that confidence with tasks will free you to practice art in nursing

- Identify what the "art" in nursing means to you

- What are your personal experiences that may help you to practice the art of nursing?

- Identify personal biases that may impede your ability to practice the art of nursing

- Understand that professional nursing is based upon science

- Define what evidence-based practice means to you

- How do you use evidence-based practice in your clinical rotations/daily practice?

- How would you articulate an evidence-based rationale for a simple task you do daily?

- What is your testable question?

CHAPTER 7

Keep Your Compassion: One Day You Will Be on the Other Side of the Gurney

For some of you this will be easy, and for some of you not so much. As you may well know, professional nursing is difficult. There are many demands placed upon the nurse throughout the workday. Multitasking is one trait you must develop. If you cannot multitask, well, we won't go there. I am assuming all of you are excellent multitaskers. If you are applying into a program, currently in a program, or you have started your first year of practice, you are realizing what I'm talking about. The rigorous demands placed upon you will never end. You will just need to adapt and develop skills that will help you cope with these endless demands. Long work hours, understaffing, high acuity patients, and the increasing complexity of care that patients require are factors that contribute to compassion fatigue. Many individuals wish to enter the field of nursing as they feel they embody traits associated with being empathetic. Many individuals wish to deliver empathetic care to patients during the most stressful times of their lives. People identify caring or advocacy traits within themselves that help them make the decision to study to become a nurse. Right?

I recall an incident prior to becoming a nurse in which I had witnessed a horrendous car accident take place literally a few feet in front of my face. I was traveling in a car with a friend and we witnessed a vehicle pull out in front of us at high speeds, and before we knew it, this vehicle was T-boned by another car. The vehicle that was T-boned flipped in mid-air. As we witnessed the impact, I could see a person being ejected out of the car into the street. This all looked as if it was happening in slow motion. I felt the rush of adrenaline course through my body, and I was compelled to respond. As our car came to a stop, I instinctively jumped out into traffic and ran toward the scene. I could hear my friend, who was actually a registered nurse, yell at me to get back into the car. I kept running toward the wreckage. I didn't know what I was going to do, but I felt compelled to do *something*. In hindsight, this was not the safest or smartest thing to do. I made no evaluation for scene safety, and I made no evaluation for my own safety. I just jumped. I am not saying you need to be a trained professional to respond and help someone in need, but you need to take into consideration your own safety before you dedicate yourself in service to others. Just because I stupidly jumped into the middle of traffic to help someone didn't make me destined for nursing school. I wasn't destined, I made a calculated decision years later. Fast forward to my first year of nursing school. What's the point of all of this? We're getting there. A particular nursing instructor was giving a lecture, and somehow the topic of CPR was brought up. A student then asked the instructor if she had ever given CPR out in the community. I was actually shocked by the instructor's response. She stated, "Listen, guys, if I ever came across someone on the floor of the grocery market turning blue, I would walk right over them (she motioned walking over an imaginary body) and call 911. You do not have to do CPR if you don't want to." Wow! What a response. I felt floored by her. What was I to make out of that response? That response resonated with me for a long time, and not in a good way. Anyway, the point is that some people are not driven by empathy and advocacy to get into the profession. Some are. Some people are empathetic and compassionate by nature and some are not. But whatever you are, you will be emotionally and physically taxed by the demands associated with professional nursing. I am not saying that the instructor I mentioned lacked empathy as a nurse. She may have been trying to emphasize that there may be legal implications for licensed clinicians intervening in a public setting. I am not sure if that was the point of her lecture, but that is a consideration.

Providing empathetic care consistently for years under stressful circumstances when meeting the overwhelming needs of patients and families during traumatic situations may result in compassion fatigue. Lombardo and Eyre (2011) note that individuals who help others in stressful situations may actually be traumatized through consistently demonstrating empathy and compassion. The nurse does not physically experience the trauma of the event that the patient suffers from but does experience the event emotionally by engaging in the care of the patient. Lombardo and Eyre (2011) emphasize that the nurse's relationship with self is essential to identifying and managing compassion fatigue. There are many symptoms associated with compassion fatigue. The identification of any one symptom may be an indication of compassion fatigue. There are work-related, physical, and emotional symptoms the individual may suffer. Some work-related symptoms may include dreading working with certain patients and a lack of joy in the work environment. This may lead to excessive sick calls. Some emotional symptoms of compassion fatigue include mood swings, anxiety, irritability, depression, anger, poor concentration, lack of judgment, and lack of focus. Individuals suffering from compassion fatigue may also exhibit physical symptoms which include fatigue, insomnia, sleeping too much, headaches, palpitations, and digestive problems (Lombardo & Eyre, 2011). Well, it appears as though I've had compassion fatigue for twenty-five years! That was a joke. But honestly, this phenomenon is not a joke, because compassion fatigue, if left unchecked, may progress into complete burnout. The nurse-patient relationship and the relationship with the patient's loved ones are at the core of delivering empathetic and compassionate care during some of the worst experiences that patients and their families will suffer in their lives. It would be in your best interest to recognize and be aware of the progression of symptoms associated with compassion fatigue. The first step to fixing anything is the acknowledgment and identification of a problem. If you are in school and feeling fatigued from your work-life balance, you may need to identify school resources that will assist you with the stressors you are experiencing. Do not internalize this stress. Just like you are learning to make care plans for patients, you need to get in the habit of making care plans for yourself. Identify school resources, friends, colleagues, and family to assist you with the delivery of your own self-care. If you are beginning your practice as a registered nurse and you're feeling overwhelmed, then you should seek help from your employee assistance program (EAP). Human resource has this program available for you. These programs provide support in relation to work-life balance issues. These programs may also provide classes that teach the individual how to utilize techniques for stress reduction. In the work environment, seek out colleagues who act as mentors to you. Seek out colleagues who understand the stressors involved in your daily work and ask for guidance in identifying strategies to mitigate the very deleterious effects of chronic stress.

Why is self-care so important? Why do you need to be able to recognize the signs and symptoms of compassion fatigue? Honestly, you will not be an effective provider if you cannot take care of yourself first. If you do not take care of yourself first and develop your own unique strategies for self-care, you will be unhappy. Do not be unhappy. You have worked for too long and too hard to be unhappy. Unofficially, a hallmark of nursing is self-sacrifice. You cannot sacrifice yourself and expect to be healthy and productive. Unfortunately, one day we will all be consumers of healthcare. I hope not, but one day you may find yourself on the other side of the gurney. And if you are, I hope that your nurse is happy, healthy, and engaged to give you empathetic and compassionate care during a scary time in your life.

Chapter 7 Key Points:

- Identify your individual traits

- Are you an empathetic person?

- Are you a compassionate person?

- How does stress affect you?

- When you physically leave work, does your mind leave work too?

- Do you ruminate on things you could have done better?

- Do you put your needs first? If not, why?

- Identify symptoms of compassion fatigue

- Do you suffer from any of those symptoms?

- If you suffer from some of those symptoms, who can you share that with?

CHAPTER 8

When You Thought
You've Seen It All

Working in a perioperative environment is an amazing experience, but after years and years of practice, sometimes it can become very routine. One particular day, it was not unlike any other workday except that I was assigned to work in the interventional endoscopy department as a PACU nurse. I thought to myself what a wonderful assignment. Unlike the surgery department, many of these cases although highly specialized, were generally quick cases, which oftentimes meant quick recoveries, high volume, and fast turnover. This scenario, to me, represented a very stress-free day. Although these cases tended to be much shorter than general surgery cases, they were still considered high acuity. After all, these endoscopy services were being facilitated in a hospital environment. These were the cases that could not be done in an outpatient surgery center due to the nature of this population's comorbidities. Oftentimes, lower acuity patients are sedated for a procedure with moderate sedation in which the nurse is responsible for administering a drug cocktail, usually fentanyl and versed. In our setting, a good 99 percent of cases needed an attending anesthesiologist to administer sedation due to the medical complexity of these patients. Surprisingly, a large portion of our sixty cases that day were what we endearingly referred to as "walkie talkies." Even with the complex nature of the intervention that was needed for these patients and considering how sick they were, they could still walk into the building; well, most of them could. That day so far was off to an excellent start. The schedule was running like a fine-tuned machine. You really do have to have an expert team to safely and effectively facilitate the interventional services of sixty human beings. The safe and expert delivery of this kind of care was largely dependent on the skills of the team at hand. It's not uncommon, with such a busy schedule like this, to encounter roadblocks that you had not anticipated. It's necessary for a team to seamlessly rebalance second by second to maintain the momentum of the machinery. Human machinery. By noon we had completed about half the scheduled cases. Yes, noon. My mind was on lunch. As I was walking by a patient that had been admitted in bay 14 to check on my own previously admitted patient next to him, I heard him tell his nurse that he felt some chest tightness, nausea, and bloating. The nurse assured the patient that after his particular intervention he may indeed feel some gas, bloating, and epigastric discomfort and that this was normal and to be expected. The nurse encouraged the patient to belch and offered an antiemetic. The nurse explained that when he was ready, she would like him to try eating some ice chips. She needed to get him to start taking some fluids by mouth so that she could start facilitating his discharge home. I half ignored the patient's complaint because his nurse was with him at the bedside and also because of the nature of this patient's intervention. It is possible for patients to feel bloated, belch a lot, and present with some mild abdominal distention. This complaint was not necessarily unusual in the context of this setting. Of course, we are all trained to examine the nature of chest tightness, right? The clinician must take into consideration the differential diagnosis for the complaint. I half glanced over to see the patient lying completely flat on his back. He just looked uncomfortable. I walked over and asked his nurse who was busy looking for discharge orders in the computer if I could help her boost him up in the stretcher and sit him up. We did that. I looked at the patient, then at the monitor. He was in a sinus rhythm in the 90s, oxygen saturation 99 percent on 2 liters nasal cannula, and blood pressure of 140s over 90s. He looked a little dusky. Breathing about twenty-four breaths per minute. I asked, "How are you doing, sir?" He stated he didn't feel good and that he felt pressure in his chest. He pointed to his epigastric area as he described the chest pressure. He was tachypneic when he spoke. Remember, he just had a fifteen-minute oral endoscopic procedure. I asked the nurse who the anesthesiologist and proceduralist were. I asked her to call them now because the patient just did not look right. The nurse responded, "He just needs to wake up. This was a very quick case, and the patient only had propofol sedation." This certainly was not a normal post-procedure presentation for this kind of case. I asked to touch the patient's stomach. It was rotund but soft. Was this his preop baseline? The patient increasingly became more tachypneic, about 26–28 respirations per minute. The oxygen saturation began decreasing to about 89 percent on 4 liters. I removed the nasal cannula and explained that I wanted to give him more oxygen. As I was putting on a simple face mask, the patient exclaimed, "I feel sick, I'm gonna throw up!" He did. A very large amount of bright red blood. The attending anesthesiologist was at the bedside now. He looked at the bright red emesis and stated, "Oh boy, that is not good, get the proceduralist." We suctioned the patient, supported his airway, and the patient continued to vomit large amounts of bright red blood. How could there be this large volume of frank blood in such a very short period of time? This necessitated not just a mere rapid response call, but we called for a code blue. The patient still had all pulses, and he was maintaining a blood pressure. At this period in time, the cuff pressure indicated that he averaged a mean arterial pressure (MAP) of greater than 80. His sinus rhythm rapidly progressed to sinus tachycardia at a rate of about 130 beats per minute. Although understandably extremely anxious, he was still completely neurologically intact and could follow commands. His tachypnea was worsening, so the anesthesiologist called for a C-MAC video laryngoscope to intubate the patient. The patient continued to vomit large volumes of bright red blood. Where was the source? We worked vigorously to clear his airway. It was difficult to see his cords with all of the blood, but the anesthesiologist was successful with intubation. By this time an entire code blue team was at the bedside, and we needed every single person. As I mentioned earlier, we were in an endoscopy lab, but we were right down the hall from our surgical suites. One of our team members had already called for a surgeon to come to the bedside. The proceduralist who did this patient's case stated that there was no obvious source of any active bleeding that he could find during the procedure. In a matter of moments, as I surveyed the bedside, it was evident that not only did we have a code blue team present but general surgeons, fellows, residents, and multiple attending anesthesiologists. This was no ordinary surgical consult. I mean, when had there ever been a stat surgical consult at the bedside of an outpatient who had a fifteen-minute oral endoscopy? The effortless and seamless synchronicity of events and team member actions involved in the work of saving this patient's life could not have been planned any better than what was actually happening in this moment.

I had been assisting with airway and intubation. A nasogastric tube was inserted, and a left radial arterial line was placed. There was a good waveform from the arterial line, which means he still had a pulse. He now had a MAP of about 60. We had already initiated our massive transfusion protocol. As I continued to survey the patient and team to identify needs that could be addressed, I glanced down at the patient's abdomen and noticed his abdominal girth was increasing. As the surgeons were at various stages of their assessment while simultaneously conferring about the hemodynamic status of the patient, I stated, "Hey, look at his abdomen." His abdomen prior to this moment was large, rotund, and soft. Now, it was evident that there had been a significant increase in his girth and his abdomen was rock hard.

Arrangements were being made with the operating room, which was literally just down the hall, to move him immediately into a surgical suite. The patient's MAP was trending down. Multiple pressors including levophed and dopamine were started. By this time, a triple lumen central line had already been placed. Our massive transfusion protocol had already been started by our operating room colleagues. They too were called to the bedside as plans were being made to move this patient to an operating suite. Despite these amazingly well-coordinated efforts, the patient's hemodynamic status was deteriorating. The patient was still bleeding out from some unknown source. Before I knew it, the operating room team was being directed to stop planning on moving the patient, even just down the hall. The patient was just too unstable to move. They were being directed to bring the operating room to us! Our PACU team continued to assist the anesthesiologists, yes, plural, *many* anesthesiologists, with titrating the pressors and other immediate tasks associated with the massive transfusion protocol that was in progress. Before we knew it, I was witnessing multiple operating room team members bringing in general surgery instruments. They began to create a makeshift sterile field right in the middle of our PACU. They surrounded the patient with the makeshift field. Their efforts were amazingly coordinated during this very unique situation. The surgery attendings and the operating room nurses began delegating to our staff what their needs were. An amazing cardiac anesthesiologist seamlessly took the helm of the case from our attending anesthesiologist. The patient was prepped and draped in a sterile fashion, and before I could actually absorb what was happening, an incision was made. The incision started below the xiphoid process and went down to below the umbilicus. The patient's abdominal cavity was opened. The surgeon gently lifted the bowel out of the abdominal cavity as he searched for a source of bleeding. The patient was continuing to bleed out with no obvious source, and the patient's hemodynamic status was worsening. We continued to titrate the levophed and dopamine to very high dosages, and we added an epinephrine drip. Multiple blood products were infusing. The surgeon decided to cross-clamp the abdominal aorta as the patient continued to deteriorate. As I looked up to the monitor, I realized the patient was becoming increasingly bradycardic. "He's brading down!" Just now, after all of these heroic and extraordinary interventions, we were fast approaching a classic code blue situation. Standard ACLS drugs were given to treat the bradycardia and drips were titrated up, but the patient still deteriorated until we were witnessing ventricular fibrillation on the monitor. The pads had already been placed on the patient, and we immediately began to defibrillate. We now were engaging in code blue protocol while the surgeon still intensely searched for a source of bleeding. I cannot convey the unsettling level of calm that this particular surgeon demonstrated as he methodically kept searching and searching for this elusive bleeder. He was unrelenting in his search just as the rest of our team was unrelenting in their interventions to save this patient. We continued with these life-saving interventions. We continued epinephrine. We continued shocking. We continued every measure to save life until the patient was in asystole, and then we continued even more. We exercised every intervention conceivable in these last moments. We, as a team, were provided with every imaginable technological and pharmacological resource to give the most comprehensive and exhaustive critical care to this patient. Finally, the code was called. The surgeon still continued to look for a source of bleeding. It was 4:30 p.m. The patient expired. He was gone. The room seemed oddly silent now as the surgeon still kept searching. I glanced at the surgical instruments that had been used. I looked around the room at all of the used blood products that had been strewn in various areas. I noted countless empty syringes and vials on the field. I looked at the patient. Someone standing next to the primary surgeon looked like he was preparing to sew up the abdominal incision. Various groups of team members were blankly reflecting upon what had just happened. The various groups just stood there, surveying the room, talking quietly among themselves. Two physicians were inquiring as to where the family was. The family had been in the waiting room the entire time, patiently waiting for their loved one to meet discharge criteria to go home. The family anticipated the nurse would call them to come into PACU to be with him as he was waking up. I looked over at the primary nurse who had been assigned this patient. She was trying to clean the patient's face. I asked to stay with that nurse so that I could help her do postmortem care for her patient. We cleaned him up in silence.

A Need for Debriefing

Unwittingly, at the beginning of this scenario, other patients were being brought out from the procedure rooms to recovery bays. Of course, we diverted those incoming patients, but eventually, it would be expected that we resume our work schedule. The patient's nurse and I continued post-mortem care. Honestly, I felt physically and emotionally exhausted, and I'm sure everybody else felt the same way too. I had experienced countless code blue situations over the past twenty-five years, but I had never participated in a code blue such as this one. This was a first. Surprisingly, I was met with another first on this day. Within forty-five minutes after this code was called, all of the team members in our unit who were directly involved in the care of this patient were being summoned to our conference room. I wondered what this was all about. As I walked into the conference room, all of our department management, operating room management, participating physicians, nurses, and operating room staff were present. I noticed a young woman in a suit at the front of the room. She introduced herself as a "clinical crisis manager." She acknowledged her role would be to facilitate this debriefing. According to Hanna and Romana (2007), debriefing is defined as an encounter based upon sharing information and processing a traumatic situation that occurred between peers. This process is explored via conversation among the peers present during the event. In addition to a code blue, a critical incident encompasses terrorism, workplace violence, industrial accidents, adverse drug reactions leading to unanticipated injury or death, and other serious events (Hanna & Romana, 2007). Ultimately, it's the discretion of the manager to recognize the need for debriefing. Well, I guess our manager anticipated that we should be debriefed after this occurrence. She made that assessment relatively quickly, I might add. I had never been invited to engage in such a process in all my years. Didn't any other managers in all those past years recognize that frontline hospital staff encounter traumatic scenarios daily throughout their careers? Anyway, the facilitator gave a synopsis of the critical incident that she was informed had occurred. Firstly, she presented an open opportunity for all involved at the table to speak up and verbalize feelings regarding this code. People very cautiously and slowly started to verbalize their perception of this encounter. My boss was sitting directly across from me. I could feel her observing *me* as I observed and listened to other staff. At first, I was thankful I was present for this debriefing and not because I wanted to share my feelings. I have rarely shared my feelings related to these kinds of situations in a work environment. I was thankful I was there because I was so physically drained, and I just wanted to sit down. We were exhausted. I didn't feel anything but tired. No emotions. Before I knew it, a very young surgical tech began to cry as she expressed her thankfulness for being able to try and help this patient. I am sure this was a first for her too. I was surprised at the level of emotions that were flowing in that room. My manager continued to stare at me. She was a nurse practitioner who also had many years of teaching experience under her belt. She was an excellent administrator and an excellent frontline staff advocate. I was also surprised that she was still an excellent clinician too. During this code, as we were multitasking hanging blood products and titrating drips, she came right to the bedside and exclaimed, "What can I do to help?" Then she started to help in any way she could find. Anyway, my manager continued staring at me during this debriefing until I finally made eye contact with her. She asked, "How do you feel, Robert?" I stared at her for a moment. Silence. Her eyes started to well up with tears. I began to speak. I commended my team members on their extraordinary and heroic efforts to try and save this life, and as I continued speaking, I felt my voice begin to crack. I was beginning to feel emotions that I did not want to feel, and my eyes began to well up with tears. And yet another first! We were all colleagues, but we did not all personally know each other. We had many operating room suites and a very large staff to boot, but in this instance, we were all connected through this experience.

I want to bring you back for a moment to the topic of work environments. We previously discussed Magnet-designated hospitals and Magnet philosophies. Hanna and Romana (2007) note that the process of debriefing can be related to the six "forces of magnetism." These forces include the quality of the nursing leadership that demonstrates compassion for staff, utilization of an open and collaborating management style, utilization of consultation and resources for staff, utilization of interdisciplinary relationships, utilization of the concept of nurses as teachers, and finally, the implementation of the concept of quality of care in the debriefing process (Hanna & Romana, 2007). You should be able to identify each of these forces of magnetism in this scenario that was presented to you.

Chapter 8 Key Points:

Phases of Debriefing:

- Introduction: Facilitator establishes trust and group goals

- Fact gathering: Staff describes what happened

- Reaction phase: Facilitator examines group feelings

- Symptoms: Facilitator examines how this event has impacted the group personally

- Stress response: Facilitator teaches the group about their response to stress

- Suggestions: Facilitator offers guidance on how to cope with stress

- Incident phase: Group identifies positive aspects of events

- Referral phase: Facilitator identifies individuals who need further support

(Hanna & Romana, 2007)

CHAPTER 9

Burnout: Beware!

Many of you reading this book may not have completed your formal education yet, and many of you may be early on in your career. The concept of burnout may seem like it is on the very distant horizon for you. Not true. You need to start identifying the root cause of this problem that many nurses will experience at some point in their careers. It could be you, so take note. Bakhamis, Paul, Smith, and Coustasse (2019) define burnout as the state of emotional exhaustion that can make an individual feel overwhelmed by their work situation. This feeling causes excessive fatigue to the point of being unable to meet work demands. Emotional fatigue impairs the ability of the individual to have meaningful engagement with others and results in cynicism and detachment from work. As this exhaustion progresses, the individual may perceive patients and colleagues as objects, and ultimately this exhaustion will make the individual ineffective at work. This kind of fatigue will also impair the individual's ability to maintain healthy relationships. Astoundingly, it is reported that the incidence of burnout in registered nurses is a whopping 70 percent (Bakhamis, Paul, Smith, & Coustasse, 2019).

Bakhamis et al. (2019) cite the United States Bureau of Labor Statistics as noting that there are currently 2.8 million registered nurses in the United States. The number of physicians and surgeons is roughly one million. As you can deduce by these numbers, the registered nurse is a critical component of the United States healthcare system, so the root cause of burnout is essential to examine.

STAFFING SHORTAGES

The modern healthcare system is driven by profit. In order for organizations to survive in a very competitive environment, these organizations must optimize the delivery of their services. As in any other business, there is great emphasis on cost containment. And yes, healthcare is a business. The United States population is aging, and life expectancy has increased. Historic programs, such as the Affordable Care Act, have given millions of people access to healthcare for the first time, and the number of RNs relative to the whole population accessing care is small. Translation? Lots of patients and not enough nurses. Even though there are roughly 2.8 million RNs in the United States, it is projected that there is a looming shortage of RNs that is fast approaching a million vacancies. This shortage is projected to become worse. It has been projected that there will be an estimated 1.2 million vacancies by 2020 and in the next ten years, a whopping 55 percent of the RN workforce aged fifty years and older will retire (Bakhamis et al., 2019). What does this mean for you? Well, that means as an RN, you will likely experience consistent staffing shortages. Unfortunately, low staffing levels, use of ancillary personnel in place of RNs, an aging population with complex and multiple comorbidities, and an organizational focus on cost containment measures equals a very heavy workload for you! Welcome to nursing. You have a solution, you say? What's that, get more nurses? Well, here's why that's not working.

According to the American Association of Colleges of Nursing (AACN, 2020), there has only been a 5.1 percent increase in enrollment in entry-level baccalaureate nursing programs in 2019. This low number is not adequate to meet the demand for nursing services, including nurse faculty and nurse researchers. This is basic supply and demand. As we explored earlier regarding entry into practice, there are plenty of associate and baccalaureate programs, but we are lacking nurse faculty, hence the infamous and perpetual waiting lists to get into certain programs. AACN (2020) notes that because of this faculty shortage over 80,000 qualified nursing school applicants were turned away due to unavailable faculty, no clinical sites, no classroom space, or clinical preceptors (American Association of Colleges of Nursing [AACN], 2020). Currently, it is reported that the average age of a registered nurse in the United States is fifty years old. This means, as emphasized earlier, that we will be grossly underprepared to meet the needs of an increasingly aging population in the next fifteen years as this cohort of nurses will retire. Yes, we are going to retire and leave it to you! As a nursing student or new nurse, you will need to be acutely aware of these current trends as they will impact your happiness in relation to work and life balance. Nursing shortages impact nurse happiness and subsequently patient outcomes. There are numerous studies that have found that the proportion of professional registered nurses at the bedside delivering care compared to utilizing nurse assistive personnel has directly impacted patient outcomes. Basically, organizations that choose to utilize assistive personnel in greater numbers than professional registered nurses will realize increases in preventable deaths, a reduction in the quality of care, and ultimately, nurse attrition. This never-ending cycle causes nursing shortages that contribute to registered nurses leaving the profession entirely. Bakhamis et al. (2019) cite a study by Konwinski that documented a nurse turnover rate of 35–61 percent within the RNs' first year of work! There are dire consequences associated with RN burnout. Research has documented that burnout is associated with poor patient outcomes, increased medical errors, increased incidence of rates of infection, and most disturbingly, an increased incidence of patient mortality. One hospital that participated in a nurse burnout study reported an estimated financial loss of $300,000 for every percentage point increase of their annual nurse turnover rates (Bakhamis et al., 2019).

STAFFING RATIOS

You have obviously heard of nurse-to-patient ratios. Nurse-to-patient ratios not only affect nurse job satisfaction but impact patient outcomes. It is worth noting that California is the only state in the entire United States of America that has mandated nurse-to-patient ratios! Go California! But how is this possible? Only one state in fifty has ratio laws that protect nurses and patients? Yes, but it must be noted that other states have staffing regulations, policies, and committees responsible for staffing plans. But again, California is the only state that stipulates in law a required minimum nurse-to-patient ratio which must be maintained at all times. This law is currently being challenged due to the ongoing crisis situation related to the COVID-19 pandemic. Well, how does this affect you and your patient? Simple, AACN (2020) notes several studies that have found higher patient loads were associated with an increased mortality rate of approximately 6 percent and higher hospital readmission rates. Ok, synthesis of all the literature on nurse-to-patient ratios would equal one common outcome. Simply put, nursing units that are perpetually understaffed equate to an increase in mortality risk for patients. How many times can I emphasize that nurse-to-patient ratios and nurse staffing are directly correlated with an increase in patient mortality? Not enough! We are talking about preventable death and poor patient outcomes, people! This could be your family member we are talking about. Know your organization's safe staffing policies and state laws.

MASLACH BURNOUT INVENTORY (MBI)

The Maslach Burnout Inventory (MBI) helps to identify the incidence of burnout by examining three dimensions which include emotional exhaustion, depersonalization, and inefficacy (Bakhamis et al., 2019). Emotional exhaustion is characterized by extreme exhaustion and fatigue that comes from constant stressful work demands. When an individual experiences depersonalization, they become insensitive to the care of patients, may lack empathy, and may objectify them. Inefficacy refers to an individual's feelings related to their own personal achievements in the work setting. The topic of registered nurse burnout is ongoing, and as of yet, there has been no resolution. This issue is of great concern as it is having a significant impact on the United States healthcare system. Burnout syndrome is a phenomenon that is experienced throughout all of the world's healthcare systems. It is not solely a domestic problem. Burnout syndrome impacts patient care, quality of care, and nurse job satisfaction. If measures are not taken to mitigate the pervasive damage this syndrome causes, there will be huge ramifications that we will all experience as consumers of healthcare. Take a self-inventory and see where you stand.

Burnout Self-Test Maslach Burnout Inventory (MBI)

The Maslach Burnout Inventory (MBI) is the most commonly used tool to self-assess whether you might be at risk of burnout. To determine the risk of burnout, the MBI explores three components: exhaustion, depersonalisation and personal achievement. While this tool may be useful, it must not be used as a clinical diagnostic technique, regardless of the results. The objective is simply to make you aware that anyone may be at risk of burnout.

For each question, indicate the score that corresponds to your response. Add up your score for each section and compare your results with the scoring results interpretation at the bottom of this document.

Questions:	Never	A Few Times per Year	Once a Month	A Few Times per Month	Once a Week	A Few Times per Week	Every Day
Section A:	0	1	2	3	4	5	6
I feel emotionally drained by my work.							
Working with people all day long requires a great deal of effort.							
I feel like my work is breaking me down.							
I feel frustrated by my work.							
I feel I work too hard at my job.							
It stresses me too much to work in direct contact with people.							
I feel like I'm at the end of my tether.							
Total score – SECTION A							

Questions:	Never	A Few Times per Year	Once a Month	A Few Times per Month	Once a Week	A Few Times per Week	Every Day
Section B:	0	1	2	3	4	5	6
I feel I deal with my team/ colleagues impersonally, as if they are objects.							
I feel tired when I get up in the morning and have to face another day at work.							
I have the impression that my team/ colleagues make me responsible for some of their problems.							
I am at the end of my patience at the end of my work day.							
I really don't care about what happens to some of my team/ colleagues.							
I have become more insensitive to people in the workplace.							
I'm afraid that this job is making me uncaring.							
Total score – SECTION B							

Questions:	Never	A Few Times per Year	Once a Month	A Few Times per Month	Once a Week	A Few Times per Week	Every Day
Section C:	0	1	2	3	4	5	6
I accomplish many worthwhile things in this job.							
I feel full of energy.							
I am easily able to understand what my team/colleagues feel.							
I look after my team/colleagues problems very effectively.							
In my work, I handle emotional problems very calmly.							

Through my work, I feel that I have a positive influence on people.							
I am easily able to create a relaxed atmosphere with my team/colleagues.							
I feel refreshed when I have been close to my team/ colleagues at work.							
Total score – SECTION C							

SCORING RESULTS – INTERPRETATION

Section A: Burnout

Burnout (or depressive anxiety syndrome): Testifies to fatigue at the very idea of work, chronic fatigue, trouble sleeping, physical problems. For the MBI, as well as for most authors, "exhaustion would be the key component of the syndrome." Unlike depression, the problems disappear outside work.

Total 17 or less: Low-level burnout
Total between 18 and 29 inclusive: Moderate burnout
Total over 30: High-level burnout

Section B: Depersonalisation

"Depersonalisation" (or loss of empathy): Rather a "dehumanisation" in interpersonal relations. The notion of detachment is excessive, leading to cynicism with negative attitudes with regard to colleagues, feeling of guilt, avoidance of social contacts and withdrawing into oneself. The professional blocks the empathy they can show to their colleagues.

Total 5 or less: Low-level burnout
Total between 6 and 11 inclusive: Moderate burnout
Total of 12 and greater: High-level burnout

Section C: Personal Achievement

The reduction of personal achievement: The individual assesses themselves negatively, feels they are unable to move the situation forward. This component represents the demotivating effects of a difficult, repetitive situation leading to failure despite efforts. The person begins to doubt their genuine abilities to accomplish things. This aspect is a consequence of the first two.

Total 33 or less: High-level burnout
Total between 34 and 39 inclusive: Moderate burnout
Total greater than 40: Low-level burnout

A high score in the first two sections and a low score in the last section may indicate burnout.

Note: Different people react to stress and burnout differently. This test is not intended to be a clinical analysis or assessment. The information is not designed to diagnose or treat your stress or symptoms of burnout. Consult your medical doctor, counsellor or mental health professional if you feel that you need help regarding stress management or dealing with burnout.

C. Maslach, S.E. Jackson, M.P. Leiter (Eds.), Maslach Burnout Inventory manual (3rd ed.), Consulting Psychologists Press (1996)

BURNOUT: POSSIBLE SOLUTIONS

As I have mentioned throughout this book, I believe that the Magnet Recognition Program is a way to improve not only outcomes for patients, but it also serves to increase work satisfaction for the nurse. Bakhamis et al. (2019) acknowledge that programs such as Magnet have documented positive outcomes related to an improved work environment, a decrease in mortality rates, and an improvement in patient care. Magnet hospitals have documented that nurse retention rates are far superior to organizations that do not engage in Magnet tenets. Nurse retention rates are superior and the quality of the professional nurse is superior because these programs emphasize the importance of exceptional work environments for their staff. Exceptional work environments include transformational leadership that is truly engaged with frontline staff issues. The emphasis of nurses as teachers and emphasis on interprofessional collaboration and collegiality truly help to reduce the incidence of RN burnout. The nationwide implementation of these programs is a good first step to decreasing the high rates of nurse burnout. Surprisingly, it is estimated that only 8 percent of US hospitals have achieved

Magnet designation (ANA, 2015). So how are the other 92 percent of US hospitals treating their registered nurses?

NURSE RESIDENCY

As a registered nurse beginning your professional practice, there will be many obstacles that you will need to overcome before you develop a level of comfort, confidence, and competence in your daily practice. New nurses are faced with a myriad of challenges that could not have been anticipated in the student environment. A new nurse that is thrown in to sink or swim without support and guidance will often sink. Without a well-structured supportive environment, a new nurse may be faced with what seems like insurmountable challenges that may potentially and rapidly progress to feelings of emotional exhaustion, depersonalization, and inefficacy (Bakhamis et al., 2019). Surprisingly, symptoms of burnout syndrome may begin to manifest in just the first year of professional practice. Lombardo and Eyre (2011) relate the benefits of engaging in a nurse residency program. Nurse residency programs are usually one year in length and offer new graduate nurses an evidence-based curriculum that is focused on new hospital orientation topics, organizational policies and resources, and issues and trends that the new graduate nurse will encounter. Generally, nurse residency programs are curriculums that meet national residency accreditation standards. These programs offer a supportive environment, structured learning, and mentorship that will help shape and develop the nurse's critical thinking skills and ultimately assist the new nurse with gaining autonomy in his or her clinical practice. These programs aim to help the new nurse transition into a fully functioning and competent staff clinician. The nurse will benefit from this type of residency program by experiencing feelings of inclusion and self-worth which are nurtured by a structured orientation process that builds confidence. This structured and supportive environment will set the nurse on a path to future professional development and success within the organization.

Self-Care, Self-Care, Self-Care

How are you going to take care of anyone else if you can't find time to take care of yourself first? No, really? Our altruism as a profession can also be the crux of the matter of burnout as well. We are programmed early on to self-sacrifice. It is drilled in our heads that we can't possibly take breaks or go to the bathroom because of the nature of our work. In a twelve-hour shift, patient needs are never-ending. It is not just a twelve-hour job but a 24/7 job, and some of us hit the gates running with just that idea in mind. We just don't stop. We just don't stop until we don't feel well ourselves. That's not good. I remember, early in my career, I constantly refused to take breaks. I felt like that was a cop-out. I felt like I was being lazy if I took a break. I felt like if I took a break, I wasn't working hard enough. Really?! I had countless things to attend to for my heart patients, and I believed that if I personally didn't do it myself, then it just would not get done right. Yeah, sure. I would never say no to a manager if I was asked to work overtime, regardless of how tired I was. Ultimately, later on in my career, I needed to take on-call responsibilities for the perioperative department I worked in. I worked a full-time schedule, and in addition to my scheduled hours, I took call approximately 100–130 hours in a two-week period. Even if I was called in to recover an emergency appendectomy at 0300 in the morning, I was still expected to return to work the next day at 0700 and be on time. I do not think that was healthy for the nurse or the patient, but that was the expectation. I carried the "no breaks" and "don't say no to call or overtime" philosophy for decades. That was not a healthy work strategy, I can assure you. As a nursing student or a nurse in your first years of practice, you will need to develop positive self-care strategies. Lombardo and Eyre (2011) note that it is essential to develop healthy rituals to prevent compassion fatigue. Healthy rituals must be developed but also maintained. Some healthy rituals include engaging in adequate nutrition and hydration, exercise, and good sleep. Remember we talked about developing a *Like List* when it came to deciding upon choosing a nursing specialty. Well, we all get so consumed with school, work, and family that we don't focus on our *Life's Like List*. Make a list of the kind of exercise you like. I know, sometimes we feel so exhausted that it's just not conceivable that we would have the energy to exercise, but you must. When you don't want to is the precise time to make yourself do it! Even if it's just walking around the block. You have got to choose a physical activity no matter how simple and commit to doing it on a regular basis. The same thing applies when it comes to your spiritual and emotional health. Find and engage in activities that fill your emotional and spiritual toolbox. You must develop self-care strategies that take your mind away from work stressors. In the beginning, when you are just starting your career, it will be difficult to say no to overtime. You might feel like you are letting your team down. Do not feel that way. Guilt is a toxic and useless emotion. Should anyone make you feel guilty about taking care of yourself first? I think not. To be of service to others, you must take care of *yourself*. There is no negotiating that. So, remember your work-life balance and learn to graciously advocate for yourself. When it comes to being overworked, "Just say no!"

CHAPTER 9 KEY POINTS:

- **Define burnout**

- **Recognize symptoms of burnout**

- **Identify the nurse-to-patient ratios, staffing guidelines, or staffing laws in your state**

- **Identify staffing guidelines in the organization where you work**

- **What is the nurse turnover rate in the organization where you work?**

- **Are these rates of turnover good or bad?**

- **What is your organization doing to address these rates of turnover?**

- Do you sometimes feel burned out?

- Take the Maslach Burnout Inventory (MBI) self-test

- Identify solutions to burnout

- Identify self-care strategies

- Make a *Life Like List*

- "Just say no!" to unhealthy work-life balance

CHAPTER 10

Rebirth: Reinvent Yourself!

You may just be getting started, but it is always wise to begin exploring the abundance of opportunities that may await you after you finish your education and complete your first year of practice. I recall a surgical tech, who I think would make an incredible nurse, ask me if she should pursue nursing. I asked her, "Well, do *you* want to become a nurse?" She confided that she did but had an aunt who is a nurse caution her not to. I asked her why her aunt said to avoid becoming a nurse. She explained that her aunt was completely unsatisfied with her chosen medical-surgical specialty. I asked how long her aunt had been practicing in med-surg. She responded, "Oh, about twenty years." Listen, folks, this is the beauty of our profession. If you are unhappy in your specialty, don't do it for twenty years. The longer you stay, the more difficult it will be to change. This holds true for anything in life. You never leave a boyfriend you don't love because you're "used" to him. You stay with an unstimulating job because you've done it for so long. You allow your wife to verbally abuse you because you can't ever imagine making a plan to leave. Listen, change is difficult, and the older you get and the longer you wait, makes it even more difficult. I explained to that surgical tech that her aunt engages in a specialty she is miserable in because that's what she has chosen to do. She may have started out there, got comfortable, and the next thing you know, twenty years have passed and she is practicing in a specialty that is not her passion.

I advised her to start filling her toolbox with knowledge and start exploring interests related to nursing via her *Like List*. Do not make a decision for your future based on one anecdotal report of misery. We are all different. Gather the evidence from multiple sources on how you personally can contribute to the nursing profession and make an impact. Find your passion, and if you are having a hard time finding it, then start working on creating it. In all honesty, nursing is a very tough profession. It would serve you to start thinking about concepts like *reinvention* now. One of my best friends who graduated nursing school with me was in complete shock during her first two years of practice. She wanted to be a nurse since she was five years old. To me, she was the epitome of what a nurse symbolized. She was kind, caring, and compassionate. In our friendship over the years, she has demonstrated such love and patience with me, and believe me with my personality, that is no easy task. I thought she would make the perfect nurse. We ended up graduating together, which was no easy task either. We passed our NCLEX-RN and happily had jobs waiting for us. I recall talking with her almost daily about our clinical experiences as newbie nurses. I started out on a step-down open-heart unit, and she started on a telemetry unit. The shock of being the new RN and not the student began to sink in! I had envisioned my friend as the perfect nurse, a guardian angel to her telemetry patients, effortlessly saving their lives and making a huge impact on all that she encountered. Well, she is a guardian angel and does make a huge impact on all she encounters, but during those first two years as a nurse, she cried to me every week about how she hated her job. She confided in me that she could not believe the disconnect from the student experience versus actually being the professional responsible for the outcomes of the patients she took care of. She had never fathomed the level of responsibility associated with being a nurse. Neither did I. She told me she cried almost every day when she would get home from work. She cried for two full years. She cried and cried and cried, until she got cancer. Non-Hodgkin's lymphoma. My friend had to take a medical leave. She was just beginning her career. She was diagnosed early, treated, and slowly reintroduced to work. Serendipitously, the same manager of the telemetry unit that she had worked in was the manager of the electrophysiology (EP) lab. The manager expressed concern for my friend's ongoing fatigue after the recent chemotherapy and suggested that during her reintro-duction to work she be trained in the electrophysiology lab. The EP lab is a high-tech environment where equipment is utilized to monitor and map the electrical conduction system of the heart. EP studies can also be used to predict the risk of sudden cardiac death. Some studies that EP nurses assist with are cardiac ablations of dysrhythmias, scrubbing for insertion of pacemakers and internal cardiac defibrillators, and providing moderate sedation for these procedures. These are just a few of the many responsibilities of the EP RN. My friend was not fully versed or completely oriented to all of the tech in that lab for a full two years after she started in that department. She ended up becoming a full-time staff member there and remained in that department for fifteen years! When we spoke about how she was doing in her new job, she gushed with joy! She loved her job. She no longer needed to cry to me every week about work. She was engaged and exhilarated serving a very specific patient population in this very unique specialty. Please do not let cancer have to help you decide to make a change for the better.

Nursing Specialties

During your clinical rotations, you were briefly introduced to different specialties. I emphasize the word *briefly*. You most likely had limited time and exposure to the various specialties you encountered but were exposed enough to those patient populations to have some understanding of whether you liked it or not. During my clinical rotations, I knew immediately that I did not want to be an obstetrics nurse. I did not want to work in labor and delivery, post-partum, psychiatry, or anything to do with pediatrics. Those clinical experiences, although absolutely necessary for my education, narrowed down the choices I needed to make. I knew immediately that I was exhilarated to work in the adult acute care environment.

I especially liked cardiac nursing, and ultimately and luckily, that's where I ended up after graduation. I say luckily because you may not get the kind of job or work in the kind of specialty that you had envisioned for yourself right away. This is why I emphasized filling up your toolbox with advanced certifications such as ACLS and PALS. Even if you end up in medical-surgical nursing, which is not a bad thing, you will have demonstrated to a prospective employer your desire to go above and beyond the requisite qualifications for an entry-level hospital job as a new nurse. Exploring the content of study involved in achieving those advanced certifications will also open you up to identifying what you like and what you don't. Those certifications will also give you a leg up when you want to transfer to an ICU or PACU. Any telemetry unit or ICU will require ACLS, and any pediatric unit, pediatric ICU, or PACU will require both ACLS and PALS. You might as well just achieve those certifications early on.

There are hundreds of nursing specialties. In the hospital setting, there is emergency nursing, critical care nursing, labor and delivery, and pediatrics, to name a few. These specialties are further classified and based upon the acuity of that particular population you are serving. There is a nursing specialization for every system in the body. Just as medical doctors are specialized, so are registered nurses. Again, a nurse is a nurse is a nurse. Definitely not! Some nurses have decided that after so many years of practice at the bedside, they wish to seek a non-clinical job. Jobs away from the bedside in the hospital may include work as case managers, infection prevention practitioners, administrators, risk management officers, informatics specialists, nurse educators, and nurse researchers. These are but a few non-clinical specializations. There are also countless organizations outside of the hospital setting that may present a multitude of opportunities for the nurse who no longer wishes to engage in bedside nursing. Some specializations in the community include public health nursing, insurance and medical claim reviewers, legal nurse consulting, nurse authors, and nurse entrepreneurs. It is never too early or too late to start thinking about reinventing your career. If you are in school, you need to explore what you like and start thinking about specialization. If you are in your first year of practice and you are finding that what you thought you loved about your current specialty no longer holds true, then you too need to think about the steps you need to follow for reinvention. Realistically, after graduating, you will need to complete at least one year of full-time work in a hospital-based acute care setting before moving on to brighter pastures. If you can move up and on before that, you're very lucky. It is pivotal to examine what you want during this first year of practice because it will impact your future outcome. Identify short term and long-term goals. Let's say that you end up in a medical surgical unit, but because of your rotations in the operating room in school following anesthesia providers, you discovered that a long-term goal is to obtain an advanced degree and become a certified registered nurse anesthetist (CRNA). That is a great goal. If you graduated with your BSN, you know that you will need to seek admission to a master's program with an emphasis on becoming a CRNA. This is an extremely competitive curriculum. There are very specific criteria for admission that you will need to meet related to your current clinical practice before you will ever be considered for such a program. So, that means you need to make very calculated and strategic moves to transfer out of the medical-surgical unit into an ICU. Good luck! Remember your toolbox with the ACLS in it? I hope you took that class because it may be statistically improbable that you would get a transfer from med-surg to ICU. There are exceptions, like gaining access through a nurse residency program, but that is the exception, not the rule. You just wouldn't have the skill set or knowledge base to make this move. I know, you desperately want to become a CRNA! But first, a telemetry or a step-down unit might be in your future. That's why getting your ACLS right away will be helpful. The type of clinical experience you have will directly impact eligibility for admission into a CRNA program. Generally speaking, you would need a full year of ICU experience before any graduate program in anesthesia would even consider you. This goes back to my somewhat controversial recommendation to go from a new nurse status directly into a nurse residency program in the ICU. It may not be easy to get a residency program in the ICU immediately after graduation, but if that were an option, you should absolutely jump on it. Especially, if you know your long-term goal is to become a CRNA. As a new nurse, if you end up on a med-surg floor or telemetry unit, the path to becoming a CRNA will be much longer. What about nurse practitioners? you ask. That's great, I say! This is also an advanced practice role. There are many different types of nurse practitioners, which include specializations in acute care, family nurse practitioner, and gerontology. Generally, it is recommended that a student who wishes to pursue becoming a nurse practitioner have clinical experience in an acute care setting. Unlike CRNA, you do not need a full year of ICU experience to qualify for entry into these programs. One controversial note of caution: There are some nurse practitioner schools that do not require *any* clinical experience for entry into the program. Yes, some of these programs will accept your brand-new BSN without any clinical practice hours as a professional nurse on the floor. I do not recommend you take this route. I am a staunch believer that you must become a competent and experienced RN before you will ever be ready to practice at an advanced level.

Registry Nursing!

In order to begin picking up registry shifts and travel contracts, you will need to have completed at least one year of full-time clinical practice in an acute care setting. This is where the concept of knowing who you are really comes into play. Do you like the status quo and mundane daily routine? Do you like the excitement of change, new environments, and new people? Registry and travel nursing offer countless opportunities to either work locally or actually take assignments outside of your home base. Registry shifts provide an excellent opportunity to explore your local environment either in the hospital or surgery center venue. When you sign up with a registry, you will need to provide a documented history (a least a year) of relevant clinical experience in your chosen specialty. Of course, you will provide all of your certifications, licensure, health documentation, etc., just as you would for a full-time employer. Registry companies have contracts with multiple hospitals and surgery centers. There is now a trend in application-based registry companies. You log into your portal, input all of your credentials and work criteria, and you will receive notifications for particular "gigs" in your area. The notice will list the specialty, the patient population, the hours, bonuses, and rates of pay. You can even negotiate a higher rate of pay than what the company listed if no one is booking the shift. Oftentimes, a last-minute shift will be posted with what they term as a "pay boost." This usually happens because one of their staff members called in sick and they need a stat replacement. So, if you are extremely flexible and adaptable, you can make a very independent living this way without the politics of being a staff nurse. You may call in daily or provide the days and times *you wish to work* to your local registry, or you can just use the application-based registry and program your work preferences and notifications. What is great about being a registry nurse is that you call the shots. No fixed schedule, days, or times. You create all of that at your whim. It is usually registry policy that you must cancel your shift within a two-hour time frame if you decide you can't make it. That is perfectly legit to do, but I wouldn't make a habit of that. You want to develop a reputation as a reliable professional. With all of these great perks, there are indeed some downsides to making a living this way. Just as you can cancel your shift with the registry, they can also cancel you last minute. There is one feature on the application-based registry that encourages employers not to cancel your shift. The application-based policy says that if an organization cancels your shift within four hours, they will pay you a penalty for cancelling you. And if you constantly cancel on them, they will review you in a negative light, which may impede your ability to book shifts. So, it's a give and take. The cancellation thing can keep you from making a specific amount of money that you had anticipated, so you will need to be super flexible and assertive to book enough shifts. Some registries will "master book" you if you desire. That is a specified block of time that you will commit to work for a unit. An example would be that a hospital anticipates there will be staff summer vacations coming up, so they need to cover those shifts for a specified amount of time. Master booking is great because you can go to a place, become adept at their charting systems, get to know an organization and the people, and then decide if you ever want to go back or take employment with them. Generally, registries furnish a higher rate of pay than a staff job would, but they do not provide comprehensive health benefits. That is why this kind of lifestyle might not work for everyone. When working registry, you will also need to deliver a high level of clinical competence and professionalism when you show up for your shift at the facility. If you do not, you may be placed on what is called a "do not send list" for that particular hospital. That is like blacklisting you from ever being utilized in the organization. Truthfully, you will need to be super competent clinically because a lot of times, you will find units that will give you the most difficult, exhausting, and daunting of assignments. Sometimes the unit culture practices the ideology that "Well, the registry nurse is making way more money than me, so give them the worst assignment." Sad but true. Fortunately, if you go there often and find you are being exposed to that culture of abuse, just do not go back. You will ultimately find assignments in units where they are so grateful to have a registry nurse because of their constant understaffing; they will treat you like gold. When you find this kind of a unit where the staff are truly appreciative of your help, then see if you can be master booked and stay a little while. Always maintain a positive, friendly, team-based approach, and you will do well.

Travel Nursing!

Travel nursing is similar to registry nursing. Not only is it a great way to explore other organizations and meet new people locally, but it will give you the opportunity to actually travel to other states you have always wanted to visit. Even other countries! I have had colleagues take year-long contracts in Saudi Arabia! If you do not want to go that far, there are plenty of opportunities in all of the great 50 states of the United States. You can also stay within your local home area and explore all of the organizations there, but the perks of your contract will be different. Oh yes, that is one distinction between registry work and travel assignments. The contract. With a travel assignment, you will commit to a certain period of time as stipulated within an actual formal temporary contract of employment. These lengths of time vary, from as little as 8-week contracts upto 16-week contracts. At the end of your contract, if they like you and you like them, you are usually provided with an opportunity to "extend," as they call it. That means you will re-sign with your company to commit to another 8-, 12-, or 16-week period. I continue to emphasize the word *commit*. Unlike registry, you cannot cancel two hours prior to your shift. You can call in sick, of course, but these contracts are more structured like full-time employment for short periods of time. This is good because you will get to know the organization, the people, the patient population, the workflow, and computer charting. Again, you will need to be an expert clinician because unlike a new employee, you will be expected to hit the ground running. I have had assignments where I was expected to be fully functional after just one twelve-hour shift! Usually, a staff person orientation would last for months. Just like registry, you may encounter some unit cultures where they will want to give you the worst patient assignment. What do I mean by the worst? Usually, that means the most difficult and the most critical. I recall a certain travel contract I had for a large urban hospital in their PACU. I worked under a very talented charge nurse. Her special skill was to ensure that I received every unstable vented patient coming out of the operating room. I honestly don't know how she did it. But she made sure that if the patient was about to code, I got the assignment. She possessed some super triage skills to make certain that my bay was full of only the most critical patients. I still gave her chocolates every day that I worked, but it never did any good. She always expected chocolate, and I always expected a vent. In hindsight, it only made me a stronger clinician, but I can tell you it also exhausted me. I ended up renewing my contract for a full year though. But the choice would be yours not to renew. Unlike registry, with these contracts, you will have a full benefits package, even if it's only an 8-week contract. You are free to negotiate your rate with multiple companies as several companies may have the same listing, and often their benefit perks are different. One thing you must understand though is that a true travel contract stipulates that you must travel at least fifty miles outside of your "tax home." Your tax home is where you live full time and where you file your taxes. This is called the fifty-mile "radius rule." This is important to understand because in a true travel assignment, you will commute at least fifty miles outside of where your permanent residence is. The reason this is important is that if you are a "true traveler," you are eligible to receive tax-free money in your check. This includes what they call a "housing stipend" that you don't pay taxes on. In addition to this tax-free housing money, you will get tax-free "per diems" for food and expenses. These are nontaxable monies that will also go into your check. The taxable monies include your negotiated rate of pay. This rate is usually reduced to below-market rates that people normally would make on a taxable job. So, your hourly rate in a travel contract will be smaller than that with a regularly taxed full-time job. This translates to much less tax being taken out of your check. When you average the combined taxable and nontaxable pay you are receiving in a travel contract, you usually end up coming out way ahead. The way they calculate the housing stipend you will receive is by local market rates. So, if you want to take an assignment in Los

Angeles, they will come up with the cost of an average rental in the area of your assignment. Let's say the company quotes you that the housing rental rate is $3,000 per month in Los Angeles. The company will either give you that $3,000 tax-free in your check in addition to your salary, or they will pay for your apartment. It's your choice. Many travelers have local friends they stay with, so they end up pocketing the housing cash. If you don't know anyone or you don't have a friend to stay with during your assignment, the travel companies usually offer amazing housing in some of the best buildings in the city where you will work. Many people who come to Los Angeles stay in some great iconic buildings located on the Sunset Strip. Housing options are offered depending on where your assignment is. Be aware that many travel companies will verify your tax home to establish that you are a true traveler. They want to verify that you are not a local and living next door to your assignment. This prevents people from posing as travelers and taking tax-free money. Don't do that. If you are not fifty miles outside of your travel assignment, then you are what is called a "local traveler." I did this for many years. You still benefit from the many travel perks discussed, but all of your pay and perks will be taxed. No tax-free money for you. People spend entire careers as registry and travel nurses. It just depends on who you are. Some people have spent their entire professional careers in one hospital on the same unit! To some, that would be unfathomable. I know a nurse who did just that. I met her in Los Angeles en route to Hawaii. She told me she dedicated her entire life to one organization and to her one daughter and exclaimed with hands in the air that it was time to reinvent herself. She took a short assignment in Los Angeles with plans on doing the next assignment in Hawaii. She said that was the beginning of her rebirth as a nurse and as a person. There are many ways to reinvent yourself in professional nursing practice. It would benefit you to start taking a self-inventory right now.

CHAPTER 10 KEY POINTS:

- Identify what you are not happy about in your current situation

- Identify short-term goals to make your change

- Identify long-term goals to make your change

- Invest in continuing education to meet your new goals

- Create new networks in other specialty areas through school or work

- Identify and create a relationship with a mentor in another specialty area

- Continue personal and professional development

- Monitor opportunities posted outside of your current environment

- Explore the local registries in your community

- Explore what a travel assignment would have to offer

CHAPTER 11

On COVID-19

At the time of this writing, we are smack-dab in the middle of the most unprecedented public health crisis our nation has ever seen. At least within the last hundred years. This pandemic has affected all of our lives in so many ways. It has touched everyone. Not only has it impacted the education and well-being of school-aged children and adolescents, but it has touched you too. Clinical rotations have been cancelled, admission into programs has been postponed, and consequently, many people's goals and aspirations have been put on the back burner. For all of you that are currently practicing, your professional work lives have been turned upside down. Many of you who work in perioperative departments have been furloughed. If you were per diem in one of those units, you might have been abruptly taken off the schedule and told to just hold on until things normalize. At the opposite extreme, many nurses were told that they would be "deployed" to other units to assist with the impending coronavirus disease 2019

(COVID-19) surge. Yes, "deployed," a word that is frequently associated with troops going off to war. Many of us in our home units were displaced to other units throughout the hospital and expected to deliver the same level of competent safe and effective care for our patients. Workflows have been stopped completely on some units, while other units have had to reinvent and optimize workflows that could have never been imagined, such as delivering care under a tent in a parking lot. In the beginning, conflicting information regarding the precise mode of transmission of the virus, i.e., droplet transmission versus airborne transmission, created a struggle for organizations to provide the best and most appropriate forms of personal protective equipment to their employees. There was a steep learning curve at the onset of this pandemic, and the learning is still in progress some ten months later.

Many of my colleagues fell ill with COVID-19 and were subsequently removed from the frontlines. This created a need for a constant replenishing of the troops, as it were. We all struggled with fear and anxiety as we faced a new unknown, but we were still bound with the duty to care for our patients even though we weren't yet sure of the best way to do it. Within the past ten months, we certainly have gotten more confident and competent in taking care of patients suffering from COVID-19. We have adapted to unusual and innovative new workflows that assist in taking care of these patients while protecting our non-covid patient populations. The organization I currently work for has a 1,000-bed capacity. During our most recent surge, we have been over our capacity. Over 1,000 beds full with approximately 450 of those beds being occupied by patients with COVID-19! This has touched every single person who reports for duty within our organization.

The CDC has published Case Fatality Ratios (CFRs) and Infection Fatality Ratios (IFRs) according to age. CFRs represent the proportion of infected individuals with fatal outcomes. CFRs include only populations with clinical symptoms. In other words, populations that are identified as confirmed cases. The IFR includes populations with clinical symptoms *and* asymptomatic carriers, which would equate to *all* infected individuals. Some experts have calculated that COVID-19's IFR is 1 percent as compared to Influenza's IFR of 0.1 percent. What does that mean? That means it is estimated that COVID-19 is ten times more deadly than the flu. Why do I emphasize this? This is important to note because not only is COVID-19 more deadly than influenza, but it also has a much higher rate of transmission. With the flu, one sick person usually infects one other person, whereas with COVID-19, one sick person can infect 2.5 people. This is called the R-naught, which represents how contagious an infection is. According to the CDC's IFR data categorized by age, the younger you are the less deadly the virus will be to you. I must caution all of you youngsters out there to take the same protective measures against this virus as everyone else. Yes, do it for your grandma but also for you. Anecdotally, I have seen countless cases of very young people hospitalized and gravely ill. One case, in particular, coming to our unit for an emergent intervention comes to mind. This was an eighteen-year-old who presented with what was described as "flu."

He had suffered from high fevers, cough, fatigue, and extreme headaches for three days at home prior to seeking care in our emergency room. Upon admission to ER, he presented with hypotension, extreme tachycardia, and altered mental status. He presented with a pattern of coagulopathy characterized by elevated fibrinogen and D-dimer levels. He was also diagnosed with myocarditis. This young man was very sick. He had no other comorbidities except that his body mass index was calculated to be greater than 30. No other medical problems. He was just 18 years old and had never been sick before. Statistically, this patient's presentation will not be common among the majority of young people infected with COVID-19, but take pause and take precautions. Just one case like this in *your* family will make an impact on your life.

No, We Didn't Sign Up for *This*

As the fatigue and exhaustion begin to set in with the overwhelming stressors involved in strategically and safely managing this pandemic on the frontline, we want to know that the general public is doing their due diligence in complying with public health and safety guidelines. As a student or a new nurse during these unprecedented times, you may have heard many in the public express that "Well, this is what you signed up for." Let me clarify this to you. COVID-19 is not a political phenomenon. Severe acute respiratory syndrome coronavirus 2 (SARS-CoV-2) is a new strain of coronavirus that causes COVID-19 disease. There is nothing to politicize about this virus and how it's transmitted. Nada! End of story. It's just science people, but it really is more than that. It's also just common sense. If you sneeze on someone's face and that person is not wearing a mask, they will be exposed to more droplets than they would be if they were wearing a mask. And if you were six feet away from that sneeze, you would be exposed to even fewer droplets. Wow, science *and* common sense! So, here it goes. We did not sign up to be overwhelmed by the "Karens" of the world who go around making a political agenda out of not wearing a mask and then end up in the hospital with COVID-19. "Karen," who is now sick in the hospital, still refuses to wear a mask as she's being transported down the hallway to a procedure room. Her non-compliance with basic containment measures poses a risk to everybody. She argues with staff about not wearing her mask and continues to spout out conspiracy theories that there is no virus. We did not sign up for that! We did not sign up to be overwhelmed by the "Karens" gone wild in the grocery store intentionally causing conflict with rational and responsible frontline workers trying to enforce public health policy. We did not sign up to be overwhelmed by a small segment of the LGBTQ community who have blatantly and egregiously ignored public health guidelines, law, and policy. This small segment of the gay community has deliberately organized maskless parties on the down low, where hundreds, if not thousands, of partiers attended and willingly engaged in the spread of COVID-19. During one of these parties, a relatively young individual contracted the disease and subsequently ended up in the hospital. He lost 100 lbs. He struggled for his life battling COVID-19. After his acute illness battling the virus, he touted himself as the poster boy for struggle and survival. During his hospitalization, he created a Go Fund Me account for all of his supporters to contribute to his recovery as he had been displaced from work. He collected tens of thousands of dollars. Six months later, he was well enough to attend another one of these super spreader parties hosted in a neighboring country. Your Go Fund Me money well spent. Go figure. We did not sign up for that!

There is no political agenda involved with the transmission of a virus, but it must be acknowledged that there have been severe financial repercussions to individuals and small business owners throughout the country as a result of individual state public health policy. Also, people have perceived that their constitutional rights have been infringed upon. This is most likely the root cause of the great divide among people who will either comply with public health mandates or refuse them. I personally believe in the "no shirt, no service" policy. So, during a pandemic, the "no mask, no service" policy is just kind of the obvious thing to do.

This novel virus has indeed presented a very steep learning curve for us all. It has exposed our strengths and our weaknesses as individuals and as a nation. COVID-19 has exposed the collective weakness and fragility of the entire US healthcare system. What we did sign up for as nurses was to make a difference in people's lives. You can do this in so many ways and on so many different levels. You may be just starting out on your path to becoming a registered nurse or you may be early in your practice, but it would benefit you to think about the bigger picture of the lives that you personally touch. I have emphasized that COVD-19 is not to be politicized, but expanding your purview regarding how policy impacts healthcare delivery will benefit you. We are educated and trained to engage in evidence-based practice. Our education includes the participation in disseminating this scientific knowledge to effect positive health outcomes for individuals, communities, and whole populations. The buck starts with you. Yes, it's all up to you and how you interpret your professional responsibilities. Our healthcare system has been broken for a very long time. We are at a pivotal point in our nation's history. The onus is on each of us individually to take steps to effect positive change. Something must be done now. You have begun this long journey. Stay strong and focused, and be mindful that your efforts, no matter how small, count. This book is a call to action aimed directly at you. Yes, *you* are the future of our healthcare in this country. Do something. In the words of a very cranky surgeon as he ran to the operating room, "Hey! If you want something to happen, *then make it happen*! Don't be passive!" He was right.

References

American Association of Colleges of Nursing website. (2020). https://www.aacnnursing.org/News-Information/Fact-Sheets/ Nursing-Shortage

American Nurses Association. (2015). *Nursing: Scope and standards of practice* (3 ed.). Retrieved from https://www.lindsey.edu/academics/ majors-and-programs/Nursing/img/ANA-2015-Scope-Standards.pdf

Bakhamis, L., Paul, D., Smith, H., & Coustasse, A. (2019). Still an Epidemic: The Burnout Syndrome in Hospital Registered Nurses. *The Health Care Manager, 38*(1), 3-10. https://doi.org/10.1097/ HCM.0000000000000243

Benner, P. (1982). From novice to expert. *The American Journal of Nursing, 82*(3), 402-407. Retrieved from https://www.medicalcenter.virginia.edu/ therapy-services/3%20-%20Benner%20-%20Novice%20to%20Expert-1.pdf

Christie, W., & Jones, S. (2014). Lateral violence in nursing and the theory of the nurse as wounded healer. *The Online Journal of Issues in Nursing, 19*(1). doi:10.3912/OJIN.Vol19No01PPT01

Hanna, D. R., & Romana, M. (2007). Debriefing after a crisis. *Nursing Management, 38*(8), 38-47. Retrieved from https://www.nursingcenter.com/ journalarticle?Article_ID=735650

Lombardo, B., & Eyre, C. (2011). Compassion fatigue: A nurse's primer. *The Online Journal of Issues in Nursing, 16*(1). doi:10.3912/OJIN. Vol16No01Man03

Magnet model. (n.d.). Retrieved February 3, 2020, from
https://www.nursingworld.org/organizational-programs/
magnet/magnet-model/

Maslach, C., Jackson, S. E., & Leiter, M. P. (1996). Maslach Burnout
Inventory Manual. In *Burnout Self Test: Maslach Burnout Inventory (MBI)*
(3rd ed.). Retrieved from https://www.monkeypuzzletraining.co.uk/
free-downloads/MBI_self_assessment_for_organisations.pdf

U.S. Bureau of Labor Statistics. (2020). Occupational outlook handbook.
Retrieved February 2, 2021, from https://www.bls.gov